I CAN JUMP PUDDLES

AUSTRALIAN CLASSICS

I CAN JUMP PUDDLES
ALAN MARSHALL

Lloyd O'Neil

First published in 1955
by F W Cheshire Pty Limited
This edition published 1972
by Lloyd O'Neil Pty Limited
337 Auburn Road, Hawthorn, Victoria, Australia
Distributed by Golden Press Pty Limited
2–12 Tennyson Road
Gladesville
NSW
Printed in Hong Kong
ISBN 85550 320 3

Preface

THIS book is the story of my childhood. In these pages I have described those influences and those incidents that helped to make me what I am.

But I wanted to do much more than record the experiences of a little boy faced with the problem of his crutches; I wanted to give a picture of a period that has passed. The men and women here described are a product of that period and they too are passing. The influences that made them self-reliant, forthright and compassionate, have given way to influences that can develop characters just as fine, but the mould has changed and the product is different.

To give a picture of life at that time, I have gone beyond the facts to get at the truth. I have sometimes altered scenes, made composite characters when this was necessary, changed time sequences to help the continuity and introduced dialogue that those who shared my experiences of the horse-days may find confusing.

I ask their pardon. A book of this nature demands a treatment that facts do not always supply; the truth it seeks to establish can only be revealed with the help of imagination.

Alan Marshall

To

My Daughters

HEPHZIBAH AND JENNIFER

who can jump puddles too

1

W HEN my mother lay in the small front room of the weatherboard house in which we lived, awaiting the arrival of the midwife to deliver me, she could see tall gums tossing in the wind, and a green hill, and cloud shadows racing across the paddocks, and she said to my father, "It will be a son; it is a man's day."

My father bent and looked through the window to where the dark, green barrier of the bush stood facing the cleared paddocks.

"I'll make him a bushman and a runner," he said with determination. "By God, I will!"

When the midwife arrived he smiled at her and said, "I thought the little chap would be running around before you got here, Mrs. Torrens."

"Yes, I should have been here half an hour ago," said Mrs. Torrens brusquely. She was a heavy woman with soft, brown cheeks and an assertive manner. "There was Ted greasing the gig when he should have had the horse in." She looked at mother, "How are you, dear? Have you had any pains yet?"

"While she was speaking," my mother told me, "I could smell the myall-wood handle of your father's stockwhip hanging on the end of the bed, and I could see you wheeling it round your head at a gallop like your father."

Father sat in the kitchen with my sisters while I was being born. Mary and Jane wanted a brother to take to school with them, and father had promised them one called Alan.

When Mrs. Torrens brought me out for them to see, I was wrapped in red flannelette, and she placed me in father's arms.

"It was funny looking down on you there," he said. "My son . . . There was a lot of things I wanted you to be able to do—ride an' that. I wanted you to have good hands on a horse. Well, that's what I was thinking. Running, of course . . . They reckoned you had good limbs on you. It seemed funny, me holding you there. I kept wondering if you would be like me."

I had not long started school when I contracted Infantile Paralysis. The epidemic that began in Victoria in the early 1900's, moved into the country districts from the more populated areas, striking down children on isolated farms and in bush homes. I was the only victim in Turalla, and the people for miles around heard of my illness with a feeling of dread. They associated the word "Paralysis" with idiocy, and the query "Have you heard if his mind is affected?" was asked from many a halted buggy, the driver leaning over the wheel for a yarn with a friend met on the road.

For a few weeks the neighbours drove quickly past our house, looking hurriedly, with a new interest, at the old picket fence, the unbroken colts in the stockyard and my tricycle lying on its side by the chaff house. They called their children in earlier, wrapped them more warmly and gazed at them anxiously when they coughed or sneezed.

"It hits you like a blow from God," said Mr. Carter, the baker, who believed that this was so. He was the Superintendent of the Bible Class and proclaimed in his weekly announcements, as he faced his pupils with a sombre look:

"Next Sunday morning at Divine Service the Rev. Walter Robertson, B.A., will offer up prayers for the speedy recovery of this brave boy sorely stricken with a fell disease. A full attendance is requested."

2

Father, after hearing of these words, stood in the street one day tugging at his sandy moustache with a nervous, troubled hand, while he explained to Mr. Carter just how I happened to catch the disease.

"They say you breathe the germ in," he said. "It's just floating about in the air—everywhere. You never know where it is. It must have been just floating past his nose when he breathed in and that was the end of him. He went down like a pole-axed steer. If he'd been breathing out when that germ passed he'd 've been right."

He paused, then added sadly, "Now you're praying for him."

"The back is made for the burden," murmured the baker piously. He was an elder of the Church and saw the hand of God behind misfortune. On the other hand he suspected the devil of being behind most of the things people enjoyed.

"It's God's will," he added with some satisfaction, confident the remark would please the Almighty. He was always quick to seize any opportunity to ingratiate himself with God.

Father snorted his contempt of such a philosophy and said, with some savagery, "That boy's back was never made for the burden, and, let me tell you, this won't be a burden either. If you want to look for burdens, there's the place to look for them." And he tapped his head with a brown finger.

Later, standing beside my bed, he asked anxiously, "Have you got any pains in your legs, Alan?"

"No," I told him. "They feel dead."

"Oh, hell!" he exclaimed, his face stricken.

He was a lean man with bowed legs and narrow hips, the result of years in the saddle, for he was a horsebreaker who had come down to Victoria from outback Queensland.

"It was the kids," he used to say. "There's no schools outback. Only for them, by cripes, I'd never have left."

He had a bushman's face, brown and lined, with sharp blue eyes embedded in the wrinkles that came from the glare of saltbush plains.

A drover mate of his, who called in to see him one day, exclaimed, as father crossed the yard to greet him, "By cripes, Bill, you still walk like a bloody emu!"

His walk was light and mincing, and he always looked at the

ground ahead of him as he walked, a habit he attributed to the fact that he came from "snake country".

Sometimes, when he had a few drinks in, he would ride into the yard on some half-broken colt and go rearing and plunging amongst the feed boxes, gig shafts, and the remains of old wheels, scattering the squawking fowls and giving high, larrikin yells:

"Wild cattle and no brands! Let them ring! Ho, there!"

Then he would rein the horse back on its haunches and, snatching off his broad-brimmed hat, would swing it round in some mock acknowledgment of applause while he bowed towards the kitchen door where mother generally stood with a little smile upon her face, a smile that was a mixture of amusement, love and concern.

Father was fond of horses, not because they were the means by which he earned his living, but because of some beauty he saw in them. He liked studying a well-built horse. He would walk round it slowly, his head on one side, looking carefully at every feature, running his hands down its front legs, feeling for swellings or scars that would show it had been down.

"You want a horse with good, strong bone, and plenty of daylight under him," he used to say, "one that stands over a lot of ground."

He thought horses were like human beings.

"Yes, it's a fact," he had said. "I've seen them. Some horses sulk if you as much as touch 'em with a whip. So do some kids. . . . Box their ears and they won't talk to you for days. They hold it against you. They can't forget, see! By hell, it's true of horses too! Use the whip on some of them and you make a jib. Look at the chestnut mare of Old Stumpy Dick's. She's tough in the mouth. And I mouthed her, mind you. It just shows you. . . . It's in her like in Stumpy. Whoever mouthed him made a proper mess of it. He still owes me a quid on that job. Well, let it go. . . . He's got nothing."

His father had been a red-headed Yorkshireman, a shepherd, who had migrated to Australia at the beginning of the '40's. He married an Irish girl who arrived at the new colony in the same year. They say he strode on to the wharf when a ship laden with Irish girls seeking work as domestics arrived in the colony.

4

"Which one of you will marry me, now?" he called out to the girls lining the rail. "Who'll take a chance with me?"

One strong, blue-eyed colleen with black hair and broad hands eyed him speculatively for a moment, then called back, "I'm willing. I'll marry you."

She lowered herself over the ship's side, and he caught her on the wharf. He took the bundle she carried and they walked away together, his hand on her shoulder as if he were guiding her.

Father was the youngest of four children and inherited the temperament of his Irish mother.

"When I was a kid," he told me once, "I caught a teamster fair behind the ear with a paddy melon—if the juice gets into your eyes it can blind you, you know. Well, this fellow went sort of half cranky and came at me with a waddy. I made for our hut yelling, 'Mum!' This bloke meant business, mind you— by hell, he did! I had nothing left when I reached the hut. I was done. But mum had seen me coming and there she was waiting with a kettle of boiling water swinging easy in her hand. 'Keep back,' she said. 'This is boiling. Come any closer and I'll let you have it in the face.' By hell! it stopped him. She just stood there with me clinging to her skirts and watched him till he went away."

Father was earning his own living at twelve. His education had been limited to a few months' schooling under a drunken teacher to whom each child attending the slab hut that served as a school, paid half a crown a week.

After he started work he drifted round from station to station horsebreaking or droving. His youth and early manhood were spent in the outback areas of New South Wales and Queensland, and it was these areas that furnished the material for all his yarns. Because of his tales, the saltbush plains and red sandhills of the outback were closer to me than the green country where I was born and grew to manhood.

"There's something in the back country," he once told me. "You're satisfied out there. You get on a pine ridge and light a fire . . ."

He stopped and sat thinking, looking at me in a troubled way. After a while he said, "We'll have to think up some way to stop your crutches sinking into the sand outback. Yes, we'll get you up there some day."

2

Nᴏᴛ long after I became paralysed the muscles in my legs began to shrink, and my back, once straight and strong, now curved to one side. The sinews behind my knees tightened into cords that tugged at my legs till they gradually bent and became locked in a kneeling position.

The painful tension of the twin sinews behind each knee and the conviction that if my legs were not soon straightened they would always remain in their locked position, worried my mother who kept calling on Dr. Crawford to prescribe some treatment that would enable me to move them normally again.

Dr. Crawford, uncertain of how Infantile Paralysis developed, had watched my mother's attempts to bring life back into my legs by massaging them with brandy and olive oil—a cure recommended by the school teacher's wife, who claimed that it cured her rheumatism—with a slight frown of disapproval, but, after remarking "It can't do any harm," left the question of my immovable legs till he had made further enquiries about the complications being experienced by victims in Melbourne.

Dr. Crawford lived at Balunga, the township four miles from our home, and would only visit patients in outlying districts when the case was an urgent one. He drove a jogging grey horse in an Abbot buggy with the hood half-raised, so that the lining of scalloped blue felt, acting as a background, presented him to the best advantage as he bowed and flourished his buggy whip to those who passed. The Abbot buggy established him as the equal of a squatter, but not the equal of a squatter who had an Abbot buggy with rubber tyres.

He was a man with a readily available knowledge of the simpler diseases.

"I can say confidently, Mrs. Marshall, that your son has not got the measles."

But Poliomyelitis was a disease of which he knew very little. He had called in two other doctors for consultation when I first became ill, and it was one of these who announced that I had Infantile Paralysis.

Mother was impressed by this doctor, who seemed to know so much, and turned to him for further information, but all he would say was, "If he were a son of mine I would be very, very worried."

"I'm sure you would," said my mother dryly and never had any faith in him from then on. She believed in Dr. Crawford who, when the other two doctors had gone, said, "Mrs. Marshall, no one can tell whether your son will be crippled or not, or whether he will live or die. I believe he will live, but it is in God's hands."

This pronouncement comforted my mother but my father reacted in quite a different way. It brought from him the observation that Dr. Crawford had now admitted he knew nothing about Infantile Paralysis.

"Once they tell you you're in God's hands you know you're done," he said.

The problem of my contracting legs was one that Dr. Crawford eventually had to face. Troubled and uncertain, he beat his pudgy fingers in a soft tattoo upon the marble top of the washstand beside my bed while he looked down on me in silence. Mother stood beside him, tense and still, like a prisoner awaiting sentence.

"Well, now, Mrs. Marshall, about these legs. . . M-m-m-m, yes. . . I'm afraid there is only one thing we can do. He's a brave boy. That's fortunate. We just have to straighten those legs. The only way is to force them down. They must be forced straight. The question is, how? The best way, I think, would be to lay him on the table each morning then press your weight upon his knees till they straighten. The legs must be pressed flat on the table. Say, three times. Yes, three would be enough, I think. Say, two on the first day."

"Will it be very painful?" my mother asked.

"I'm afraid so." Dr. Crawford paused, then added, "You will need all your courage."

Each morning when my mother laid me on my back on the kitchen table, I looked at the picture of the frightened horses that hung upon the chimney above the mantelpiece. It was an engraving of a black horse and a white horse crowding together in terror while a jagged streak of lightning projected out of the dark background of storm and rain and hung poised a few feet in front of their distended nostrils. A companion picture on the opposite wall showed them galloping madly away, their legs extended in rocking-horse fashion and their manes flying.

Father, who took all pictures seriously, sometimes stood looking at these horses with one eye half closed to aid his concentration while he assessed their value as hacks.

Once he told me: "They're Arabs all right, but they're not pure. The mare's got windgalls, too. Look at her fetlocks."

I resented any criticism of these horses. They were important to me. Each morning I fled with them from jagged pain. Our fears merged and became a single fear that bound us together in a common need.

My mother would place her two hands upon my raised knees then, with her eyes tightly closed so that her tears were held back by her clenched lids, she would lean her weight upon my legs forcing them down till they lay flat upon the table. As they straightened to her weight my toes would spread apart then curve down and round like the talons of a bird. When the sinews beneath my knees began to drag and stretch I would scream loudly, my eyes wide open, my gaze on the terrified horses above the mantelpiece. While my toes were curving round in their agonised clutching, I would cry out to the horses, "Oh! horses, horses, horses . . . Oh! horses, horses . . ."

3

Tʜᴇ hospital was in a township over twenty miles from our home. Father drove me there in the brake, the long-shafted, strongly-built gig in which he broke in horses. He was very proud of this brake. It had hickory shafts and wheels, and he had painted a picture of a bucking horse on the back rail of the seat. It wasn't a very good picture and father was in the habit of excusing it with the explanation, "He hasn't quite got into it, see. It's his first buck and he's off balance."

Father put in one of the young horses he was handling and tied another to the shaft. He held the shafter's head while mother placed me on the floor and climbed in. When she had seated herself she lifted me up beside her. Father kept talking to the horse and rubbing his hand along its sweating neck.

"Steady, boy! Whoa, there! Steady now!"

The antics of unbroken horses never scared mother. She sat with an unconcerned expression upon her face while stubborn horses reared, came down on their knees or bounded off the road, grunting with the violence of their exertions to rid themselves of the harness. She sat on the high seat, bracing herself to every plunge or sway, one hand clutching the nickel rail at the end. She would lean forward a little when the horses backed violently or be jerked back against the seat when they plunged forward, but she always retained a firm grip on me.

"We're right," said mother, her arm firmly around me.

Father released his hold on the bit and moved back to the step, slipping the reins through his hand, his eyes on the shafter's head. He placed one foot on the round, iron step and grasped the edge of the seat, paused a moment calling, "Steady there!" to the restless, nervous horses, then suddenly swung himself into the seat as they reared. He loosened the reins and they plunged forward, the colt tied to the shaft by a halter pulling sideways, its neck stretched, as it bounded awkwardly along beside the harnessed horse. We shot through the gateway with a scattering of stones and the grating, sideways skid of the iron-shod wheels.

· Father boasted that he had never once hit the gate posts in his bounding departures, though splintered grooves hub-high in the wood suggested otherwise. Mother, leaning over the mudguard so that she could see the gap between hub and post, always made the same remark: "You'll hit one of those posts one of these days."

Father steadied the horses as we bounced on to the metal roadway from the dirt track that led to our gate.

"Steady now!" he called, then added for mother's benefit, "This trip'll take the gas out of them. The grey is by The Abbot. All his get are the same—they're always on the bit."

The warm sun and the noise of the wheels on the roadway sent me to sleep, and the bush and paddocks and creeks moved past us, veiled for a moment in the dust stirred by the feet of our horses, but I did not see them. I lay with my head against mother's arm till she woke me three hours later.

The gig wheels were crunching the gravel in the hospital yard and I sat up, looking at the white building with its narrow windows and strange smell.

Through the open doorway I could see a dark, polished floor and a pedestal bearing a bowl of flowers. But there was a hush about the building, a strange quietness that frightened me.

The room into which my father carried me had a padded

seat running round the wall and a desk in one corner. A nurse sat at the desk and she asked father a lot of questions. She wrote his answers in a book while he watched her in the way he would have watched an untrustworthy horse that had its ears back.

After she had left the room taking the book with her, father said to mother, "I never come into one of these places without feeling like telling them all to go to hell. They strip the feelings from a man like you skin a cow; ask too many questions. They make you feel you shouldn't be here as if a bloke's trying to put something over them, or something. I don't know . . ."

After a little while the nurse returned with a wardsman who carried me away after mother had reassured me that she would come in to see me when I was in bed.

The wardsman was dressed in brown. He had a red, lined face, and looked at me as if I wasn't a boy but a problem. Carrying me into a bathroom he lowered me into a bath of warm water. He then sat on a stool and began to roll a cigarette. After he lit it, he said to me, "When did you last have a bath?"

"This morning," I told him.

"Aw, well, just lie down in it. That'll do."

Later, I sat up in the cool, clean bed in which he had placed me and pleaded with mother not to go. The mattress on the bed was hard and unyielding and I could not gather the blankets into folds about me. There would be no warm caves beneath these blankets nor channel pathways for marbles, winding about on the quilt. There were no protecting walls close to me and I could not hear the barking of a dog nor the noise of a horse munching chaff. These belonged to my home and at that moment I wanted them desperately.

Father had already bade me goodbye but mother lingered. She suddenly kissed me quickly and walked away, and that she could do this was to me incredible. I did not see her leaving me of her own will but leaving me because of some sudden, monstrous circumstance over which she had no control. I did not sing out to her or beg her to return, though this was what I longed to do. I watched her go, unable to make any effort to prevent her.

The man in the next bed watched me in silence for a little while after mother had gone, then asked, "Why are you crying?"

11

"I want to go home."

"We all want that," he said, then he turned his gaze to the ceiling and sighed and said, "Yes, we all want that."

The ward in which we lay had a polished floor, light brown between the beds and down the centre, but dark and shining beneath the beds where the feet of nurses never disturbed the covering of wax.

The white, iron bedsteads facing each other in two rows along the walls, stood on thin legs resting on castors. For a few inches around each castor the floor was bruised and dented with these little wheels that spun round distractedly when nurses moved the bed.

The blankets and sheets were drawn tightly round each patient then tucked in beneath the mattress so that they formed a binding across him.

There were fourteen men in the ward. I was the only child. After mother left me some of these men called out to me and told me not to worry.

"You'll be all right," a man said, "we'll look after you."

They asked me what was wrong with me and when I told them, they all discussed Infantile Paralysis, and one man said it was murder.

"It's bloody murder," he said. "That's what it is. It's bloody murder."

This remark made me feel important and I liked the man who said it. I did not regard my illness as being serious, but as a temporary inconvenience, and in the days that followed I met the painful periods with resentment and anger that quickly turned to despair when the pain was prolonged, but once the pain stopped it was quickly forgotten. I could not sustain a depressed state of mind for very long. There was too much to interest me in my surroundings.

I was always pleasantly surprised to see the effect my illness had on those people who stood beside my bed looking down at me with sad faces and who saw my sickness as some terrible calamity. It established me as a person of importance and kept me contented.

"You're a brave boy," they said, bending down and kissing me then turning away with mournful expression.

I used to puzzle over this bravery which was attributed to me by those I met. To be described as brave, I believed, was to be decorated. I always felt impelled to change my expression when visitors called me brave, the pleased expression that was natural to me being inadequate to carry the description.

But I was always afraid of being found out and it began to embarrass me to accept these tributes to my courage, tributes which I knew I had not earned. The sound of a mouse gnawing behind the skirting boards of my room always frightened me and I was frightened to go out to the tank to get a drink at nights because of the dark. Sometimes I wondered what people would think if they knew this.

But people insisted I was brave, and I accepted this attitude with some secret, though guilty, pride.

In a few days I identified myself with the ward and the patients and began to feel superior to new patients who entered the ward awkwardly, confused with the rows of watching faces, homesick and longing for a familiar bed upon which to sink.

The patients talked to me, using me as a butt for their jokes, patronising me, as adults do children, and calling out to me when subjects for conversation evaded them. I believed everything they told me and this amused them. From the security of their long experience they looked down on me, imagining that because I was guileless I was incapable of understanding references to myself. They spoke about me as if I were deaf and could not hear their words.

"He believes everything you tell him," a youth across the ward explained to a newcomer. "You listen. Hey, Smiler," he called to me, "there's a witch down the well near your place, isn't there?"

"Yes," I said.

"There you are," said the youth. "He's a funny little beggar. He'll never walk, they tell me."

I thought the youth was a fool. It amazed me that they imagined I would never walk again. I knew what I was going to do. I was going to break in wild horses and yell "Ho! Ho!" and wave my hat in the air, and I was going to write a book like *The Coral Island*.

I liked the man in the next bed. "We'll be mates," he said to me not long after I arrived. "How'd you like to be mates with me?"

"Good," I said. Because of the coloured picture in one of my first books I had an idea that mates should stand together holding hands. I explained this to him, but he said it wasn't necessary.

Each morning he would raise himself on his elbow and say to me, emphasising each word with a beat of his hand: "Always remember, McDonald Brothers Windmills are the best."

I was pleased that now I knew what make of windmill was the best. Indeed, this statement became so fixed in my mind that, thereafter, it always affected my reaction to windmills.

"Does Mr. McDonald and his brother make them?" I asked.

"Yes," he said. "I'm the original McDonald. I'm Angus."

He suddenly sank back on his pillow and said petulantly, "God only knows how'll they manage with me away—orders and that. You've got to keep your eye on things." He suddenly called out to a man across the ward, "What's the paper say about the weather today? Do they reckon there's going to be a drought or not?"

"The paper hasn't come yet," the man said.

Angus was the tallest and biggest man of the twelve patients in the ward. He was suffering from some complaint that caused him pain and sometimes he would sigh loudly or swear or give a deep groan that frightened me.

In the morning, after a restless night, he would say to no one in particular, "Aw, I had a hell of a night last night!"

He had a large, clean-shaven face with deep creases joining his nostrils to the corners of his mouth. His skin was smooth like tanned leather. He had a flexible, sensitive mouth that easily broke into a smile when he was not suffering pain.

He used to turn his head on the pillow and look at me for long periods in silence.

"Why do you take so long to say your prayers?" he asked me once, then in answer to my look of astonishment, he added, "I've watched your lips moving."

"I have to ask a lot of things," I explained to him.

"What things?" he asked.

I became confused, and he said, "Go on. Tell me. We're mates."

I repeated my prayers to him while he listened, gazing at the ceiling, his hands clasped on his chest. When I had finished he turned his head and looked at me. "You haven't left anything out. You've given Him the lot. God'll think a hell of a lot of you by the time He's listened to all that."

His comment made me feel happy and I decided I would ask God to make him better too.

The long, involved prayer I repeated each night before I went to sleep was the result of an increasing number of requests I was making to God. My needs grew greater each day, and as I only dropped requests when they were answered the new pleas were so far in excess of those that were answered that I began to dread the necessity of going through it again and again. Mother had never allowed me to miss Sunday School and from her I had learnt my first prayer which was a little composition beginning, "Gentle Jesus meek and mild", and which ended with the request to bless various people, dad included, though in my heart I always felt he didn't need blessing. But later, when looking at a perfectly good cat that someone had thrown away, I became frightened at its rigid stillness and was told that it was dead. In bed at nights I thought of mother and father lying still with lifted lip like the cat, and I prayed with anguish that they mightn't die before me. This was my most earnest prayer that could never be missed.

After further consideration I decided to include Meg, my dog, in a request to preserve her till I became a man and was old enough to stand her death. Feeling troubled that I might be demanding too much from God I added that, as in the case of Meg, I would be satisfied if both my parents lived till I was a man of, say, thirty. I felt that at this great age I would be past tears. Men never cry.

I prayed to be made better, always adding that, if He didn't mind, I would like to be cured before Christmas, two months away.

The pets I kept in cages and in enclosures in our backyard had to be prayed for, since, now that I couldn't feed them or change their water, there was always the danger of this being forgotten. I prayed that this might never be forgotten.

My corella, Pat, an irascible old cockatoo, had to be let out of his cage each night for a fly round the trees. Sometimes neighbours complained about him. On washing days he would land on their clothesline and pull out the pegs. Angry women, seeing white sheets lying in the dust, threw sticks and stones at Pat, and I had to pray that they would never hit and kill him.

I also had to pray to be made a good boy.

After Angus had commented on my prayers he asked, "What sort of chap do you think God is? What does He look like?"

I always pictured God as a mighty man dressed in a white sheet like an Arab. He sat on a chair with His elbows on His knees looking down at the world, His eyes darting rapidly from person to person. I never associated Him with kindliness, only with severity. Jesus, I thought, would be kind like dad, but would never swear like him. The fact that Jesus only rode donkeys and never horses was disappointing to me.

Once dad, after removing a pair of new boots he had been "breaking in", slipped on his Gillespie's Elastic Sides and exclaimed with feeling, "These boots were made in heaven." Thereafter, I believed that Jesus wore Gillespie's Elastic Side boots.

When I had finished explaining these things to Angus he commented that maybe my picture was closer to it than his was.

"My mother always spoke in Gaelic," he said. "I always saw God as a stooped old man with a white beard, surrounded by a lot of old women knitting and talking in Gaelic. God always seemed to have a patch over one eye, and mother would say, 'It's them there larrikins throwing stones.' I couldn't imagine God doing anything without first consulting mother."

"Did your mother smack you?" I asked him.

"No," he replied reflectively. "She never smacked us kids but she was very severe with God."

To a patient who said something to him from a bed on his left hand side, he answered, "You needn't worry. I won't destroy his faith. He'll think it out for himself when he's a man."

Though I believed in God and devoted part of my evening to addressing Him I regarded myself as being independent of Him. He could quite easily have offended me so that I would never have spoken to Him again. I was frightened of Him because He could send me to be burnt in hell-fire. The Superintendent of our Sunday School had described this. But more than hell-fire I feared becoming abject.

When Meg got staked in the shoulder while chasing a rabbit I felt that God had let me down badly and resolved that in the future I would look after Meg's welfare myself and blow God. I didn't pray to Him that night.

Whenever father mentioned God he criticised Him, but I liked father's attitude since it established him as someone upon whom I could rely if God failed me—he had bound up Meg's shoulder. But his manner, when God was mentioned, sometimes troubled me.

Once when he took a mare to Old Waddy Dean's stallion, Waddy asked him what colour he would like the foal to be.

"I know a way of making it any colour I like," Waddy boasted.

"Can you make it a colt or a filly?" father asked him.

"Ah, no!" said Waddy piously. "Only God can control the sex."

To me, who was listening, father's reaction to this statement seemed to question God's power over horses, though it left me with a great faith in father. Men like father, I thought, were stronger than any God.

But men in hospitals were different from men out of hospitals. Pain robbed them of something, something I valued but could not define. Some called out to God in the night and I did not like it. I felt that they should not have to do this. I did not like to admit to myself that men could experience fear. When you became a man, I thought, fear and pain and indecision just didn't exist.

In the bed to my right was a heavy, awkward-moving man whose hand had been crushed in a chaffcutter. During the day he walked round the ward talking to the patients, going messages for them, or bringing them things they needed. He advanced upon you with a large, wet smile, leaning over the bed in a fawning way. "You all right, eh? You want anything, eh?" His manner disturbed me; maybe because his kindness, his offers to help, sprang not so much from a natural compassion as from fear. There was a danger of him losing his hand, but God was good and would surely look after those who helped the sick.

Mick, the Irishman in the bed across the ward, always waved him away from his bed in a friendly way.

"He's just like a water dog," he said once when the patient was out of the ward. "Every time he comes near me I feel like throwing him a stick to bring back."

In bed he was restless, tossing, sitting up and lying down again. He patted his pillow, turning it this way and that and frowning at it. When night came on he took from his locker a little prayer book. The expression upon his face changed and his body suddenly became still. He brought from some inner reserve a suitable seriousness in which he clothed himself like a garment.

Around the wrist of his crushed and bandaged hand he had wound a chain bearing a small crucifix. He raised this metal cross to his lips and pressed it there with a still intensity. He must have felt he was not sufficiently devout in his reading because two deep lines appeared between his brows and his lips moved slowly forming the words he read.

One night, Mick, after watching him for a moment, evidently felt that this man's piety emphasised his own lack of it.

"Who does he think he is?" he said, looking towards me.

"I don't know," I said.

"No one can say I neglected the faith," he muttered, looking hard at one of his fingernails. He bit it, then added, "Not often, I haven't."

He suddenly smiled. "There was my old mother now—God bless her. A finer woman never lived, though I say it myself. Yes, it's a fact. Others'll tell you that. Ask anybody round Borlic. They all knew her. I used to say to her on the fine mornings, 'God is good, mum,' I'd say. 'Ah, yes! but the devil ain't bad, Mick,' she'd say. Yes, they don't breed them that way now."

Mick was a short, alert, nuggety man who loved talking. He had hurt his arm in some way and was allowed to get out of bed and go to the bathroom each morning. When he returned he would stand beside his bed looking down on it while he rolled up the sleeves of his pyjamas as if he were going to sink a posthole, then he would clamber in, prop pillows at his back, rest his hands on the turned-down sheet in front of him and look round the ward with a pleased expression of anticipation upon his face.

"He just sits there waiting for someone to start him off," was how Angus described it.

Sometimes Mick would look at his arm with a puzzled frown and say, "I'm damned if I can understand it! There it was right as rain, then I heaves a bag of wheat on the dray and it goes on me. You can never tell what's wrong with you till it comes on you sudden like."

"You're lucky," commented Angus. "Two or three more days and you'll be down in the pub. Did you hear about Frank?"

"No."

"Well, he died."

"Get out! Fancy that now!" exclaimed Mick. "It just shows you. One minute you're running round happy as Larry: the next minute you're cold. He was all right when he left on Tuesday. What happened him?"

"He collapsed."

"This collapsing's bad the way it gets you," said Mick, and became silent and gloomy till the breakfast tray arrived; then he brightened up and said to the nurse handing it to him, "Tell me now, is there a chance of you ever falling in love with me?"

The nurses with their white, starched aprons and pink frocks, their scrubbed hands smelling of antiseptics, went swiftly by my bed on their flat-heeled shoes, sometimes smiling at me as they passed or stopping to tuck in my blankets. Since I was the only child in their charge they mothered me.

Father's influence led me into sometimes seeing people as horses, and as I watched the nurses going up and down the ward they seemed like ponies to me.

On the day father brought me to the hospital, he had given a quick glance over the nurses—he liked women—and commented to mother that there were some good shafters among them but they were all shod wrong.

When I heard trotting horses going past the hospital I thought of father and I could see him sitting on a horse that reared and plunged and he was always smiling. He wrote me a letter and in it he said:

"It's keeping dry up here and I've had to start feeding Kate. There's whips of feed on the creek flats yet, but I want to keep her in good nick for you when you come back."

When I read the letter I said to Angus McDonald, "I've got a pony called Kate," then, repeating father, "She's a bit ewe-necked but she's honest."

"Your old man breaks in horses, doesn't he?" he asked me.

"Yes," I said. "He's easy the best rider in Turalla."

"He dresses flash enough," muttered McDonald. "I thought he was out of a buckjump show when I saw him."

I lay thinking over what he said, wondering whether it was against father or for him. The way father dressed pleased me. His clothes suggested he was a man who moved quickly. When I helped him put the harness away, the neatsfoot oil left marks on my clothes and hands, but it left no mark on father. He took a pride in his clothes. He liked his moleskin trousers to be white and unmarked and his boots were always shining.

He liked good boots and regarded himself as a judge of leather. He was always proud of the boots he was wearing—generally elastic sides. When he took them off as he sat in front of the kitchen stove each night, he would examine each one carefully, flexing the sole with his hands and pressing the upper this way and that, searching for signs that his boots were beginning to wear.

"The upper in this left boot is better than the one on the right," he told me once. "Funny, that. It'll go before the left one."

He often talked about Professor Fenton who ran a buckjump show in Queensland and had a waxed moustache. The professor wore a white silk shirt and a red sash and could do a double "Sydney Flash" with a stockwhip. Father could crack a whip but not like Professor Fenton.

While I was thinking about these things he came walking down the ward to see me. His steps were short and quick and he was smiling. He held one arm across his chest where, beneath his white shirt, something bulky was concealed. Standing beside my bed he looked down at me.

"How are you, son?"

I had been feeling contented but he brought with him the atmosphere of home and I suddenly felt like crying. Before he came, the old post and rail fence upon which I used to stand to watch him handling horses, the fowls, the dogs, the cats—all these had moved away beyond my immediate interest but now they seemed close and real to me and I needed them. I needed mother, too.

I didn't cry but father, looking down at me, suddenly tightened his lips. He thrust his hand within his open shirt where he had been holding something to him and suddenly pulled out a struggling thing of soft brown. He lifted the blankets and pushed it beneath them against my chest.

"Here, hold this against you," he said fiercely. "Clutch that to you. It's one of Meg's pups. It's the pick of the bunch and we're calling it Alan."

I wrapped my arms around its warm, snuggling softness and held it to me, and my need passed from me in a breath. I felt a surge of pure happiness and, looking into my father's eyes, I passed it on to him, for he smiled at me.

The pup moved against me and I looked down beneath the arch of blankets I had formed with my lifted arm and there it lay with its bright eyes watching me, and, seeing me, it wriggled with a quick friendliness. The eager life of it moved into me, refreshing and strengthening me so that I felt no weakness at all. Its weight upon me was good and it smelt of home. I wanted to hold it forever.

McDonald, who had been watching us, called to Mick walking down the ward with a towel across his arm, "Keep the nurses talking out there, Mick," and to father, he said, "You know what they are—dogs in here. . . . No understanding. . . . That's the trouble."

"That's so," said father, "five minutes'll do him. It's like a pot to a thirsty man."

4

I RESPECTED men. I regarded them as capable of overcoming any difficulty, of possessing great courage. They could mend anything; they knew everything; they were strong and reliable. I looked forward to the time when I would grow up and be like them.

It seemed to me that father was typical of all men. In those periods when he acted in a way I considered unusual for a man, I felt he did so consciously and that his object was to amuse people. I was sure that, on such occasions, he was always in control of his actions.

This explained why I was not afraid of a drunken man.

When father was drunk, which was rarely, he still retained, I imagined, a perfectly sober and grown-up side to the character he was presenting to onlookers even though he did not reveal it.

When, on arriving home from a prolonged visit to a pub, he flung his arm round mother's waist and, with a "Ho there!" swung her round the kitchen in a wild dance lit with whoops, I watched him with delight. A drunken man was a romping, talking, laughing man who staggered for the fun of it.

. One night two nurses came into the ward guiding between them a drunken man that the police had brought to the hospital. I looked at him in astonishment, afraid of what had happened to him, for he was being directed by something within him he could not control. Tremors shook him and his tongue was loose in his open mouth.

As he was led through the open door he looked up at the ceiling and shouted, "Hallo. What are you doing up there? Come down and I'll have a go at you."

"There's nothing up there," said one of the nurses. "Come on."

He was a prisoner walking between them. He went blundering towards the wall like a blind horse, but they guided him into the bathroom.

When they had bathed him and put him into his bed next to Mick's the sister gave him some paraldehyde. He made strange noises when he swallowed it and cried out, "Hell!" then added plaintively, "That's crook. That's terrible crook stuff."

"Lie down now," the sister ordered. "Nothing will touch you here. You'll soon be asleep."

"The coppers tried to tack it on to me," he muttered. "Me mate came at me first. . . . Well, yes, that's right. . . . Where the hell am I? You're a nurse, aren't you? Yes, that's right. . . . How are ya? We been on the booze for weeks. . . . I'll lie down. . . . I'll go quiet. . . ."

The sister, with her hand on his shoulder, pushed him gently back on to the pillow, then went away.

When she had closed the door he lay quietly for a moment in the half dark then sat up stealthily and looked at the ceiling. Then he looked at the walls and the floor beside him. He felt the iron framework of his bed as if he were testing the strength of a trap.

He suddenly noticed Mick resting on his pillows watching him.

"Goodday," he said.

"Goodday," replied Mick. "You've been in the rats, have you?"

"Rats is right," said the man shortly. "What do they slug you in this joint for the night?"

"It's on the house," said Mick. "You're jake."

The man grunted. He had full, sagging cheeks covered with a greyish bristle. The flesh around his eyed was swollen and inflamed as if he had been crying. His nose was large and fleshy, pitted with sunken pores, dark-centred, as if each of them clasped the root of a hair.

"I might know you," he said to Mick. "Ever been to Mildura? Ever been on the Overflow, Piangle, Bourke . . .?"

"No," said Mick, reaching into his locker for a cigarette. "I've never been up that way."

"Well, I don't know you then."

He sat staring ahead of him, his hands moving purposelessly

upon the bedclothes. Suddenly he whispered urgently, "What's that over there? Look! Near the wall! It's moving!"

"It's a chair," said Mick glancing at it.

The man lay down quickly and pulled the blankets over his head. His bedclothes were shaking.

When I saw him do this I too lay down and put my head beneath the blankets.

"Hey!" I could hear McDonald speak to me but I did not move.

"Hey, Alan!"

I pulled the blankets away from my face and looked at him.

"It's all right," he assured me. "He's been on a bender and he's got the D.T.'s."

"What's that?" I asked him, my voice shaking a little.

"Too much booze. He's seeing things. He'll be right tomorrow."

But I could not go to sleep and when the night nurse came on I sat up to watch her as she walked down the ward.

"Come here, sister," the man called to her. "I want to show you something. Bring a candle here."

She walked over to his bed, holding her lantern high so that she could see him. He had pulled back his blankets and was holding his finger tight against his naked thigh.

"Look! I've got it here. Look!"

He lifted his finger and the nurse, bending forward with the light of the lantern full on her face, gestured impatiently. "It's a freckle. Go to sleep."

"It's no freckle. Look, it's moving."

"Go to sleep," she said, giving him a friendly pat on the shoulder.

She pulled the blankets over him. She was so calm and unconcerned that it comforted me. In a little while I was asleep.

When I woke up in the morning I lay for a moment thinking sleepily of the eggs in my locker. I had counted them the day before but, with my mind still bemused with sleep, I couldn't remember how many were there.

Breakfast in the hospital was a meal patients ate without enjoyment.

"You eat it to keep alive," Angus explained to a new arrival one day. "You couldn't eat it for any other reason."

It consisted of a plate of porridge and two thin slices of bread bearing a scraping of butter. Those patients who could afford to buy eggs or had friends or relatives with fowls kept a supply of eggs in their locker. They treasured these eggs and became concerned when there were only one or two left.

"I'm getting low in eggs," they would say, peering frowningly into their lockers.

Each morning a nurse walked down the ward carrying a basin.

"Come on. Hand out your eggs. Who's having eggs for breakfast?"

Patients would sit up hurriedly at the sound of her voice and lean towards their lockers, some stiffly and painfully, others weakly with drawn faces, and they would open the cupboard doors and reach in for the brown paper bags or cardboard boxes that contained their eggs. They would write their names upon the eggs they intended giving her then sit hunched forward in their beds looking around them as they nursed their eggs in the grey dawn light like sad birds in their nests.

It was necessary to write your name on the eggs you gave the nurse for disputes often occurred and a man with a supply of large, brown eggs might claim he was given a pullet's egg when, after cooking, they were returned to their owners. There were some patients who took pride in the freshness of their eggs, and they would sniff suspiciously at the ones returned to them and argue they had received the staler ones of another patient.

Those patients who did not have any eggs always watched this morning ceremony with wistfulness that was sometimes resentful. Then they lay back and sighed or complained about the bad night they had had. Many patients shared their eggs with these unlucky ones.

"Now, here's three," Angus might say to the nurse. "One is for Tom over there, and one for Mick. The other's mine. I've marked them all. And tell the cook not to hard-boil them."

The eggs were always returned hard-boiled. No egg cups were provided and you held the warm egg in your hand while you gouged into it with a spoon.

Mother sent me a dozen eggs a week and it delighted me to be able to call to a man across the ward, "I'm putting in an egg for you this morning, Tom." I liked to see the smile on his

25

face when I told him this. My dozen eggs went very quickly; then Angus would give me one of his eggs each morning.

"You hand out eggs like a Buff Orpington," he used to say. "Hang on to some of them. I'm getting short."

I was trying to work out what patients didn't have eggs when I suddenly thought of the new arrival who now, when it was light, did not seem so frightening. I sat up quickly and looked across to his bed but he was hidden beneath the blankets.

"What's he doing now?" I asked Angus.

"He's still seeing things," answered McDonald, who was unwrapping a small piece of butter he had taken from his locker. "He was crook last night. He got out of bed once. Mick said he's as weak as a cat this morning."

Mick was sitting up and yawning, accompanying his yawn with a doleful cry. He scratched his ribs and said, answering Angus, "He's weak all right. No wonder. . . . The cow kept me awake half the night. How did you sleep, Mac?"

"No good. I've got that pain again. It's got me licked. It can't be my heart because it's on the right side. I told the doctor but he didn't say what it was. They tell you nothing."

"It's a fact," said Mick. "I've always said there's no one feels the pain like yourself. I rolled on my arm last night and had the devil's own job to stop from yelling out. This bird here," he nodded towards the new patient beneath his blankets, "thinks he's crook. Well, he had a hell of a good time getting crook. I'll swop my arm for his guts any day."

I liked listening to this talk in the morning but often had difficulty in understanding what was said. I always wanted to know much more.

"What did you roll over on your arm for?" I asked Mick.

"What for!" exclaimed Mick in surprise. "What do you mean 'What for'? How the hell do I know. I rolled on it because I thought it was my good arm. You're a funny little beggar, you are."

The man in the bed beside him groaned and Mick turned and addressed the mound of bedclothes.

"Yes, you're done, brother. You're going to push up daisies tomorrow. All good things come to an end, more's the pity."

"Don't say that to him," protested Angus. "You'll frighten hell out of him. Do you want an egg this morning or not?"

"Make it two and I'll pay you back next week when me old woman visits me."

"She mightn't bring you any."

"And she mightn't at that," said Mick nodding his head resignedly. "It's a funny thing but a man never marries a woman as good as his mother. I've seen it scores of times. Women today are all the same. They're going back; anyone will tell you that. You go into my old mother's pantry back home now. Hell! A mouse couldn't push his way through the jars of pickles and jams and bottles of sauce and hop beer—all made with her own two hands. You ask any woman today to make you a pot of jam . . ." He gestured contemptuously, then added in a change of tone, "She'll bring in the eggs. Give me two. I'm hellish hungry this morning."

The drunk suddenly sat upright and flung back the blankets as if he were going to leap out of bed.

"Hey! Pull 'em over you again," ordered Mick. "You played up enough last night. Stop there. They'll strap you down if you bolt now."

The man pulled the blankets back and sat clutching at his hair. He stopped and said to Mick, "I can taste that medicine yet. Everything's jumping."

"Do you want an egg?" I called out to him in a quavering, uncertain voice.

"The kid over there wants to know if you want an egg for breakfast," Mick informed him.

"Yes," he said still holding his hair. "I'll have it. I'll have it. I've got to get me strength back."

"He'll have it," Mick called to me. "Shove it in."

I suddenly liked the man and decided to ask mother to bring me enough eggs for him too.

After breakfast the nurses hurried from bed to bed replacing the quilts they had removed the previous evening. They leant over each bed, the patients looking up at them from their pillows. The eyes of the nurses, as they concentrated on the movements of their hands, were not aware of the patients. They tucked in the bedclothes, smoothed them, patted them into creaseless bindings in preparation for the matron's tour of inspection.

Some of the nurses, if they were not in a hurry, would joke

with us. Some of them were friendly, comfortable persons who gossiped with the patients and called the Matron an "old hen", and whispered "Look out!" when the sisters came through.

One of these, Nurse Conrad, a dumpy little girl who often chuckled when she was talking to the patients, was a favourite of Angus's. He always kept an orange for her when anybody gave him some.

"There's a kind little girl, now," he said to me one day when she smiled at him as she passed. "I'll shout her to see 'the Blanche Family', blowed if I don't!"

This travelling troupe of "Instrumentalists and Master Entertainers" were on their annual visit to the town and the exciting posters announcing them had already been discussed by the patients.

"There's one thing I'll say about the Blanche Family," announced Mick, "they give you a run for your money. There's a bloke there . . . He was there last year and I'm tellin' ya, he's good. . . .This bloke played 'She Wore a Wreath of Roses' on beer bottles, and hell! he brought the tears to your eyes. And only a little bloke. . . . Nothing to him. . . . You'd meet him in a pub and never notice him. By cripes, I'm sorry I'm missing it!"

The morning after they appeared Nurse Conrad, hurrying into the ward in the dawn light, was greeted by Angus, eager for news of her outing.

"Well, how did you get on?" he called to her.

"Oo! It was beaut," she said, her plump cheeks shining from her morning bath. "We had a second front seat."

She paused for a moment to glance at the report book which rested on a desk near the doorway then hurried over to Angus where she began straightening his bedclothes while she told him about it.

"It was wonderful," she said enthusiastically, "and it was packed to the doors. The man who took the tickets at the door had a black cape on lined with red."

"That'd be old man Blanche," called Mick from across the ward. "You can bet he'd be hanging round the dough."

"He wasn't old." Nurse Conrad was indignant.

"Well, his son, then," said Mick. "It's all the same."

"Go on," said McDonald.

"Did a little bloke there play 'She Wore a Wreath of Roses on beer bottles?" Mick wanted to know.

"Yes," Nurse Conrad told him impatiently. "But he played 'Home Sweet Home' this time."

"Were there any good singers there?" asked Angus. "Did they sing any Scotch songs?"

"No, none of those. There was a man there—you'd scream at him—he sang 'The Hob-nail Boots That My Father Wore'. He had us in fits. And there was a Swiss man, all dressed like a Swiss and everything, he yodelled but . . ."

"What's yodelled?" I asked.

I had been leaning over the side of my bed trying to get as close as I could to Nurse Conrad so that I could hear all she said. To me this concert was as exciting as a circus. Just to have seen the man with the red-lined cape would have been a wonderful experience. Nurse Conrad now seemed a glamorous and interesting person as if seeing the concert had endowed her with qualities she had not possessed before.

"A man who can sing up high like," she turned and told me quickly before continuing her story to Angus. "I knew a boy in Bendigo. He was tall and everything . . ." She chuckled and pushed a loose strand of hair beneath her cap. "This boy—I don't care what anyone says—could yodel as good as this Swiss man. You know, Mr. McDonald, I went with him and I could listen to him all night. I'll tell you what, I can't sing at all but I sing a lot to amuse myself, and, though I say it myself, I know a lot about music. I studied for seven years and I should know something. I loved last night, knowing about music and that. But this yodeller wasn't near as good as Bert, I don't care what anyone says."

"No," said McDonald flatly, "that's right." He seemed as if he didn't know what to say next. I wanted him to keep asking her questions but she turned and began tidying my bed. She bent over me and her face came close to mine as she tucked the edge of the blankets beneath the mattress.

"You're my boy, aren't you?" she said looking into my eyes and smiling.

"Yes," I said tensely, unable to turn my gaze away and suddenly feeling I loved her. I was overcome with nervousness and couldn't say any more.

Acting on some impulse she bent and kissed my forehead then gave a little laugh and moved across to Mick, who said to her, "An' I could do with a little bit of that myself now. I'm a child at heart, they tell me."

"You, a married man, talking like that! What would your wife say? I think you must be a bad man."

"Well, yes, an' I'm that too. I've no time for good men at all. The girls don't like 'em either."

"They do so." Nurse Conrad was indignant.

"No," said Mick. "They're like kids. When my sister's kids do anything wrong their mother says, 'You're growing like your uncle Mick.' And they think I'm the best bloody uncle of the lot."

"You mustn't swear like that."

"No," said Mick agreeably. "I mustn't. That's right."

"Now, don't crease your quilt. The matron is making her rounds early today."

The matron was a stout woman with three black hairs sprouting from a mole on her chin.

"You'd think she'd pull 'em out," Mick observed one day after she had left the ward. "But women are cranky that way. Once they pull 'em out they reckon they're owning up to having them. So they hang on to them and pretend they're not there. Aw well, let her have 'em! She'd still win a Weight for Age even if she does carry a penalty."

The matron walked swiftly from bed to bed closely followed by a respectful nurse who volunteered information about the patients she thought the matron should know.

"His wound is healing nicely, Matron. We have put this patient on to senega."

The matron believed in cheering the sick.

"A few bright words work wonders," she used to say, speaking the last three words with separate emphasis as if she were repeating a tongue twister.

Her uniform was always stiffly starched and dictated her way of moving so that sometimes she gave the impression of being animated by strings pulled by the nurse behind her.

When she finally appeared in the doorway the patients had finished their morning talk and were sitting or lying in some mood of expectation though subdued by the severity of their unrumpled beds, and brooding on their illnesses.

When Mick mentioned the matron, it was with irreverence, but now, as she approached his bed, his attitude was nervously respectful.

"How are you this morning, Bourke?" she asked with designed cheerfulness.

"Fine, Matron," Mick responded cheerfully, but was unable to sustain it. "That shoulder's crook but it's coming good, I think. I can't lift my arm properly yet. Is that anything serious like?"

"No, Bourke. The doctor is quite satisfied."

She smiled at him and moved away.

"A hell of a lot of satisfaction you get from her," muttered Mick sourly when she was out of hearing.

When the matron reached my bed she assumed the attitude of one about to say amusing and comforting things to a child for the purpose of impressing the adults listening. It always made me uncomfortable as if I were being pushed on to a stage and told to perform.

"Well, how is the brave little man this morning? Nurse tells me you often sing in the morning. Will you sing for me one day?"

I was too confused to answer.

"He sings 'Sh! Sh! Go out black cat'," said the nurse who had moved forward. "He sings so nicely, too."

"I think you will be a singer one day," said the matron. "Would you like to be a singer?"

She did not wait for me to answer but turned to the nurse and continued, "Most children want to be an engine driver when they grow up. My nephew is like that. I bought him a toy train and he is so fond of it, the pet."

She turned to me again, "Tomorrow you'll go to sleep and when you wake up your leg will be in a lovely white cocoon. Won't that be nice?" then to the nurse, "His operation is at 10.30. Sister will attend to his prep."

"What's an operation?" I asked Angus when they had gone.

"Oh, they mess around with your leg . . . fix it up . . . Nothing much. . . . They do it while you're asleep."

I could see he did not want to explain it to me and a feeling of fear touched me for a moment.

Once when father had left a young horse standing in the brake, the reins tied to the rim of the strapped wheel, while he went in to get a cup of tea, it had plunged and snapped the tightened reins and bolted through the gate leaving the smashed brake piled against the post as it galloped away free.

Father, who had dashed out at the sound, stood surveying the wreckage for a moment, then turned to me—I had followed him—and said, "Well, blast it, anyway! Let's go and finish our cup of tea."

I thought of this for some reason when Angus paused and made no further explanation. It came to me like a deep breath.

"Well, blast it, anyway!" I said.

"That's the spirit," said Angus.

5

D R. ROBERTSON, who attended me, was a tall man who always wore his Sunday suit.

I divided clothes into two groups—Sunday clothes and those you wore the rest of the week. You could sometimes wear your Sunday suit during the week but only on special occasions.

My Sunday suit was a coarse, blue serge that came in a brown, cardboard box. It was wrapped in tissue paper and had a wonderful new smell.

But I didn't like wearing it because I had to keep it clean. Father didn't like his Sunday suit either.

"Let's get this darn thing off," he'd say after returning from church, a place he rarely went to, and only then because mother insisted.

I was amazed that Dr. Robertson wore his Sunday suit every day. Not only that, I counted them and found he had four Sunday suits so I concluded he must be very rich and live in a house with a lawn. People who had a lawn in front of their house or drove a rubber-tyred jinker or an Abbot buggy were always rich.

One day I said to the doctor, "Have you an Abbot buggy?"

"Yes," he said, "I have."

"Has it got rubber tyres?"

"Yes, it has."

After that I always found it difficult to talk to him. All the people I knew were poor. I knew the names of rich people and had seen them driving past our place but they never looked at poor people or spoke to them.

"Here comes Mrs. Carruthers," my sister would yell, and we would rush to the gate to see her go past, a groom driving her pair of grey horses.

It was like seeing the Queen go by.

I could understand Dr. Robertson talking to Mrs. Carruthers but I could never get used to him speaking to me.

He had pale, sunless skin, darkening on the cheeks where the razor had slid over the sunken roots of his beard. I liked his eyes which were light blue with wrinkles around them that folded when he laughed. His long, narrow hands smelt of soap and were cool when he touched you.

He pressed my back and legs and asked me if it hurt, then he stood erect and looked down at me and said to the sister, "Severe curvature there already. The muscles on one side of his back are badly affected."

After he had examined my leg he patted my head and said, "We'll soon straighten that." And to the sister, "A re-alignment of his thigh bone is necessary." His hand moved to my ankle and he continued, "The sinews here will have to be shortened and the foot lifted. We'll cut them in front of the ankle."

He moved his finger in a slow stroke just above my knee.

"We'll do the alignment here."

I always remember the movement of his finger since it marked the line of the scar I was to bear.

The morning before he operated on my leg he paused as he was passing my bed and said to the matron, who was accompanying him, "He seems to have adjusted himself quite well; doesn't brood at all."

"No, he's quite a bright little fellow," said the matron, then added in a cheering-the-sick voice, "He sings 'Sh! Sh! Go out black cat', don't you, Alan?"

"Yes," I said experiencing the confusion that always came to me when she addressed me in this fashion.

The doctor looked at me reflectively for a moment then suddenly stepped forward and pulled back my blankets.

"Turn over so that I can look at your back," he ordered.

I turned over and for a moment felt his cool hands move down my curved spine in a questing way.

"Good!" he said raising himself and holding the blankets aloft so that I could turn over again.

When I faced him once more he rumpled my hair and said, "Tomorrow we will straighten that leg of yours," then he added, smiling at me in a way I thought was strange, "You are a brave boy."

I accepted his tribute without any feeling of pride, wondering what made him say it and wishing he knew what a good runner I was. I considered telling him but he had turned to "Daddy" who was grinning up at him with his toothless gums as he sat in his wheelchair.

Daddy belonged to the hospital like a cat belongs to a home. He was an old-age pensioner with paralysed legs and he propelled himself round the ward, or out on the verandah, in a wheelchair that had a circular rail attached to the spokes. Daddy's thin, wiry hands would clutch these rails and turn the wheels with quick thrusts. He leant forward in the chair as he propelled himself rapidly down the ward and I envied him and saw myself dashing round the hospital in such a chair and, later, winning chair races at sports meetings and calling out, "Take your lap," like bike riders.

Daddy always took up his position beside my bed during the doctor's visit. He watched the doctor eagerly as he moved round the ward, keyed and ready to say something he had prepared to impress the doctor when he stopped in front of him. It was no use speaking to him at such times; he wouldn't hear you. Yet, at other times, he talked continually.

He was an old pessimist and complainer and didn't like having to bath each day.

"The Eskimos don't wash, and you couldn't kill them with an axe," he'd say in defence of his attitude to water.

The sister put him in the bath each day and he regarded this as bad for the chest.

"Sister, don't put me under that squirty thing again or I'll get pneumonia."

He had a face that shut into folds when he closed his mouth. His domed head was sparsely covered with fine, grey hairs, too thinly covered to hide his scalp which was shiny and blotched with brown.

He repelled me a little, not because of his appearance, which I found interesting, but because I thought he was rude, and because the way he spoke sometimes made me feel uncomfortable. Once when he said to the sister, "Sister, I have had no overflow of the guts this morning. Does it matter?" I looked quickly at the sister to see her reaction but her face didn't change.

His complaints irritated me and I thought that sometimes he should say he felt good instead of always saying he felt bad.

"How are you, Daddy?" Mick sometimes asked him.

"Never been worse."

"You're not dead yet, you know," Mick would reply cheerfully.

"No, but the way I am it will be any tick o' the clock now, any tick o' the clock." Daddy would shake his head mournfully and propel himself over to the bed of some newcomer who had not yet grown tired of his moaning.

He respected the matron and was always careful not to offend her mainly because she had the power to send him away to some old men's home.

"You don't last no time at all in them there places," he told Angus, "that's if you're sick. Once you're old and crook the quicker the govmint gets rid of you the better they like it."

So he always spoke to the matron as agreeably as he could, anxious to placate her and to say things that suggested he was suffering from serious complaints that warranted him stopping at the hospital.

"Me heart feels as dead as mutton in me guts," he told her once when she asked him how he was.

I got a picture of a butcher's block with a severed heart lying damp and cold upon it and I felt depressed and said to Angus, "I am well today. I feel very well today."

"That's the stuff," he said, "keep up the good work."

I liked Angus.

That morning when the matron was making her rounds, she said to Daddy, who had wheeled his chair to the front of the fire that warmed the ward, "Who crushed these curtains?"

The open window they covered was near the fireplace and the breeze had been wafting them towards the fire.

"I did, Matron," admitted Daddy. "I thought they might blow in the fire."

"Well, your hands must have been filthy," she said angrily, "you've left black marks all over them. Always ask the nurse to tuck them back in the future."

Daddy noticed me listening and later he said to me, "You

know, the matron is a beautiful woman. She saved my life yesterday but I think she's upset about the curtains, but, you know, if I had been in my own hut I'd have done the same with my curtains. You can't be too careful with fires."

"My father has seen a house burnt down," I told him.

"Yes, yes," he said impatiently, "he would . . . The way he walks down the ward you'd reckon he's seen the lot. The flames catch hold of the curtains and away she goes—that's how it happens."

Sometimes a Presbyterian Minister visited Daddy. This dark-clothed man knew Daddy when the old fellow lived in a hut by the river. After Daddy had been taken to hospital the Minister continued visiting him and brought him tobacco and copies of the *Messenger*. He was a young man with an earnest voice and backed away like a nervous horse when any nurse revealed an intention to talk to him. Daddy was anxious to get him married and offered him to several of the nurses. I had always listened without much interest to Daddy's praise of the man and to the reaction of the nurses when Daddy suggested they marry him, but when he put the proposition to Nurse Conrad I sat up with a sudden feeling of apprehension, anticipating she would accept the old man's offer.

"*There's* a nice single man for you," Daddy told her. "He's got a nice place—mightn't be too clean, but, still, you could clean it up. You've only got to say the word. He's a clean-living bloke, of course . . ."

"I'll think about it," Nurse Conrad promised him. "Perhaps I'll go and look the place over. Has he got a horse and gig?"

"No," said Daddy. "There's nowhere to keep a horse at his place."

"I want a horse and gig," said Nurse Conrad lightly.

"I'm going to have a horse and gig some day," I called out to her.

"All right, I'll marry you." She smiled at me and waved her hand.

I lay back suddenly feeling excitingly old and full of responsibility. I had no doubts that now Nurse Conrad and I were engaged to be married. I adjusted my expression until I thought it resembled that of a brave explorer looking across the sea. I repeated in my mind several times, "Yes, we'll charge it to your account." I always associated this remark with being grown up. I often repeated it to myself when I wanted to feel a man instead of a little boy. I must have heard it one day when I was out with father.

The rest of that day I thought out plans for getting a horse and gig.

After Dr. Robertson had left me, he said to Daddy, "How are you this morning Daddy?"

"Well, Doctor, I'm bound up as if I'm sanded. I reckon I should be drenched. Do you think a dose of salts 'd shift me?"

"I think it would," said the doctor gravely. "I'll order you some."

The doctor crossed the ward and stopped beside the bed of the drunk who was sitting waiting for him, his face with its twitching mouth stamped with anxiety.

"And how are you?" asked the doctor dryly.

"I've still got the shakes a bit," said the man, "but I'm good. I think I could go out this afternoon, Doctor."

"I don't think you are quite clear in the head yet, Smith. Weren't you stark naked in the ward this morning?"

The patient looked at him in a stupefied way and then said in quick explanation, "Yes, that's right. I did that. I got up to wash my feet. I was terrible hot round the feet. They were burning."

"Maybe tomorrow," said the doctor shortly. "You may be able to leave tomorrow. I'll see."

The doctor walked briskly away and the patient sat leaning forward plucking at the bedclothes with his fingers. He suddenly lay down.

"Oh dear!" he moaned. "Oh dear me!"

After Dr. Robertson had left the ward, mother, who had been waiting, was allowed to come in and see me. I felt shy and embarrassed as she walked towards me. I knew she would kiss me and I regarded this as a bit sissy. Father never kissed me.

"Men never kiss," he told me.

I regarded displays of affection as a weakness. But I would have been disappointed if mother had not kissed me.

I had not seen her for a few weeks and she looked a new mother to me. Her smile, her comfortable figure, the fair hair that was coiled into a bun at her neck—all these were so familiar to me that I had never noticed them before; now I looked at her, noting these things with pleasure.

Her mother had been an Irish woman from Tipperary and her father a German. Her father had been a gentle and kindly man who had come to Australia with a German band in which he played the bassoon.

She must have resembled her father. She had his colouring. She had a pleasant expression and wore her character upon her face for all to see.

The wind and rain of many a winter's drive in the open brake had left fine lines upon her weathered face, a face that cosmetics had never touched, not because she did not believe in them but because she never had the money to buy them.

When she reached my bed she must have noticed my embarrassment because she whispered, "I'd like to kiss you but there are too many looking so we'll pretend I have."

When father visited me the conversation was dominated by him even though he was a good listener, but with mother I always took charge.

"Did you bring plenty of eggs?" I asked her. "There's a poor man here with no eggs. When he looks at a chair it moves."

Mother looked across at the man—I had glanced at him as I spoke—and said, "Yes, I've brought you a lot."

Then she felt in her bag and said, "I've brought you something else too," and she brought out a brown paper parcel tied with string.

"What is it?" I whispered excitedly. "Let me see. I'll open it. Give it to me."

"Please," she prompted me, withholding the parcel.

"Please," I repeated, holding out my hand.

"Mrs. Carruthers sent it to you," she said. "We haven't opened it, but we're all waiting to see what is in it."

"How did she bring it?" I asked taking the parcel and placing it on my knee. "Did she come to the house?"

"She drove up to the front gate and handed it to Mary and she told Mary it was for her little sick brother."

I tugged at the string, trying to break it. Like father, I grimaced when putting effort into my fingers. He always did it when opening a pocket knife. ("I got it from my mother.")

"Dear me! what a face you're pulling!" mother said. "Here, give it to me. I'll cut it. Is there a knife in your locker?"

"There's one in mine," said Angus who had been watching us. "You'll find it near the front, I think. Just open that drawer there."

Mother found his knife and after she had cut the string I slipped off the paper wrapping impressively addressed to "Master Alan Marshall" and looked excitedly at the lid of a flat box featuring pictures of windmills and barrows and waggons made from perforated strips of metal. I lifted the lid and there lay the strips and beside them, in smaller compartments, were screws and screwdrivers and spanners and wheels. I could hardly believe it was mine.

The toy was impressive but the fact that it came from Mrs. Carruthers was unbelievable.

It could almost be said that Mrs. Carruthers was Turalla. She had built the Presbyterian Church there, the Sunday School, the new wing of the Manse. The annual school prizes were donated by her. All the farmers were deeply in debt to her. She was President of "The Band of Hope", "The Bible Class", and "The League of Australian Women". She owned Mount Turalla, Lake Turalla, and all the best land along Turalla Creek. She had a specially padded pew in the Church with a special hymn book bound in leather.

Mrs. Carruthers knew all the hymns and sang looking up a little. But she sang "Nearer my God to Thee" and "Lead Kindly Light" in alto and for these she kept her chin down and looked stern because she had to go down very low.

When the Minister announced these hymns father would mutter into the hymn book, "Here she goes." Mother didn't like him saying this.

"She has quite a good voice," she told him once when we were having our Sunday dinner.

"It's good," said father. "I'll give her that. But she'll tag along behind the field and still pip the lot of us on the post. She'll break down if she keeps that up."

Mr. Carruthers was dead but, according to father, when he was alive he was always protesting against something. When he protested he raised a pudgy hand and cleared his throat.

He protested against cows on the road and the decline in manners. He also protested against father.

Mr. Carruthers's father, representing an English company, had landed in Melbourne in 1837 and made west from that town in bullock drays laden with stores. It was said there was rich volcanic land awaiting settlement in the open forest country a hundred miles or more away, though the Blacks were considered unfriendly and would have to be dealt with. The party had rifles for this purpose.

Mr. Carruthers eventually took up hundreds of square miles of rich land that, now divided into scores of farms all mortgaged to the estate, brought in a large income in interest alone.

The large bluestone mansion he had built on a picked site was eventually inherited by his son and on the son's death it became the property of Mrs. Carruthers.

The enormous house stood in the centre of thirty acres of parkland, a large area of which was laid out in gardens designed in English style with ordered pathways and formal flowerbeds blooming under strict direction.

In the shade of elms and oaks, and sheltered by shrubs brought out from England, pheasants, peacocks, and strange coloured ducks from China pecked and scratched in the leaf mould left from autumn fallings. A man in gaiters moved amongst them, his raised gun occasionally bursting into sharp reports as he shot at the rosellas and red lories that came in to eat the fruit on the orchard trees.

In the spring, snowdrops and daffodils flowered amidst the dark green of Australian bracken and gardeners wheeled laden barrows between the hollyhocks and phlox. Their sharp shovels, striking at the tufted grass and the heaped twigs and leaves rising to the base of the few remaining gums, severed the roots of surviving greenhoods and Early Nancies and they toppled and fell and were carried away in the barrows to be burnt.

And the thirty acres were clean and smooth and orderly.

"The Blacks would never know it now," my father said to me when we were driving past the gate one day.

From the gateway to the homestead a gravelled drive wound between rows of elm trees. Just inside this gateway a small cottage, "The Lodge", housed the gatekeeper and his family. At the sound of trotting horses or the grating of carriage wheels on the gravel he would hurry from his house and swing open the gates and raise his hat to those who entered. Visiting squatters driving Abbot buggies and pairs, city visitors in leather-sprung carriages, ladies with thin waists sitting stiffly in phaetons, looking over the heads of prim little girls and boys poised on the edges of seats facing them—they all went past the gatehouse and nodded or smiled patronisingly or ignored the gatekeeper and his raised hat.

Half-way up the drive was a small fenced enclosure. Once tall bluegums had lifted their naked limbs high above the kangaroo grass and emu bush that grew there but now dark pines shaded it and the ground beneath them was padded with brown needles.

A red deer walked ceaselessly round the enclosure, following a worn track that skirted the fence. Sometimes it raised its head and bellowed hoarsely, and carolling magpies ceased their song and flew hurriedly away.

Across from the enclosure were the stables, large, two-story, bluestone buildings with lofts and stalls and feed bins hollowed from the trunks of trees. On the stone cobbles that surrounded the buildings grooms hissed in English fashion as they curry-combed the horses that stamped restlessly, flicking their docked tails in a useless attempt to rid themselves of flies.

A wide roadway led from the stables to the portico of the homestead. When a visiting Governor or an English gentleman and his lady came up from Melbourne to experience station life and see the "real Australia" their carriages would stop beneath the portico while they alighted; then their grooms would drive the carriages down the wide approach to the stables.

On these nights the Carruthers would hold a ball in the big house and, from a bracken-covered hill behind the mansion where a clump of wattles had escaped destruction, the more daring or wistful of Turalla's residents would stand looking down at the vast, lighted windows behind which women in low-cut gowns and carrying fans bowed to their partners in the opening of the Waltz Quadrilles. The music would come up to this little group of people and they would not feel the cold. They were listening to a fairy story.

Once when father stood with them holding a half-empty bottle, he began to give a happy whoop at the end of every swing in the set they were dancing behind the lighted windows and he wheeled round the wattles with the bottle as a partner, whooping to the music.

After a while a stout man wearing a gold watch chain from which hung a gold-mounted lion's claw, a mounted miniature of the man's mother and several medals, came out to investigate the whoops.

He ordered father away and when father continued whooping he swung a punch at father. In explaining what happened afterwards, father would say, "I sidestepped him then came in quick and played up and down his ribs with the good old one-two-three like a xylophone. The wind that came out his mouth nearly blew my hat off."

When father was helping the man to his feet and brushing his clothes, he said to him, "I thought you had too many gee-gaws about you to be any good."

"Yes," said the man vaguely. "Too many . . . Yes, yes . . . I feel slightly dazed . . ."

"Have a drink," said father handing him the bottle. After the man drank he and father shook hands.

"He was all right," explained father afterwards. "He'd just got in with the wrong mob."

Father broke in most of Carruthers's horses and was friends with Peter Finlay, the head groom. Peter often visited our place and he and father discussed articles in the *Bulletin* and the books they had read.

Peter Finlay was a remittance man and could talk on anything. All the Carrutherses were poor talkers. Their reputation for brains was based on their ability to say, "Hm, yes," or "Hm, no," at the right times.

Peter could talk quickly, with enthusiasm, and people listened to him. Mr. Carruthers often said that Peter's gift for talking intelligently was the result of good breeding and that it was unfortunate he had come down in the world.

Peter didn't think he had come down.

"My old man lived according to ritual," he told father. "A hell of a ritual it was too. I had a hard job breaking away from it."

Mr. Carruthers found it difficult to entertain the important people he invited to his home. His evenings with these visitors were full of long, uncomfortable silences. A visiting Governor or a titled Englishman was not impressed by "Hm, yes," or "Hm, no," so Mr. Carruthers always sent down to the stables for Peter, when his guests were men of importance who expected their brandy to be drunk in an atmosphere of discussion.

When Peter received Mr. Carruthers's message he immediately made for the big house where he entered by a back door. In a small room reserved for the purpose was a bed with a damask quilt and upon the bed, neatly folded, was one of Mr. Carruthers's best suits. Peter would put the suit on, then present himself at the Drawing Room where he would be introduced as a visiting Englishman.

At the dinner table his conversation delighted the guests and gave openings for Mr. Carruthers to say "Hm, yes," or "Hm, no," in an intelligent manner.

After the guests had retired Peter would take off Mr. Carruthers's suit and go back to his room behind the stables.

Once he came to father and told him that Mr. Carruthers would like father to put on an exhibition of riding for the benefit of some important visitiors who were staying at the station and were anxious to see something of real Australia.

At first father was resentful at the suggestion and said, "To hell with them," but after a while he reckoned he'd do it for ten bob.

"Ten bob's ten bob," he reasoned. "You can't just turn your back on it."

Peter thought this would be satisfactory to Mr. Carruthers even if it was a bit high.

Father was undecided as to what "real Australia" was, though he told Peter that if people wanted to see it they would find it by looking in his pantry. Sometimes father thought that poverty was the real Australia but he only thought this when he was sad.

On the day he was to present himself at Carruthers's he tied a red handkerchief round his neck and put a cabbage-tree hat on his head and rode a bay mare called Gay Girl who would buck if you touched her flanks with your heels.

She was sixteen hands and could jump like a kangaroo, so when the visitors were all nicely seated on the wide verandah, sipping drinks, father appeared galloping through the trees like a bushranger and whooping in a wild, frightening fashion.

"I come round the bend to the five-bar gate flat out," he said, when telling the story. "The take-off isn't bad—a bit of gravel but enough dirt for a grip. I steady her till her stride is balanced then put her at it. I've always said a grass-fed horse'll give you all you want in a burst. I'd only brought Gay Girl in and she is fresh as paint. Well, she takes off too soon, of course—being fresh, see—but, anyway, she's going to clout, I can see that; the gate's swung high—you could walk under it. They reckon, you know, that Carruthers'd sack a bloke for putting up a scraping gate. I wouldn't put it past him."

He gestured contemptuously then went on:

"When I feel Gay Girl lift I go up with her to save her as much weight as I can—you could've shoved your head between me and the saddle as she rises. It's her front legs I'm worried about though; once they're over I'm with her all the way.

"Hell, that horse could jump! S'elp me Bob! she gives a twist and gets another two inches from the air. It don't stop her clouting with her back legs but she's in her stride two bounds from where she lands, and I'm sitting on her as snug as a brand.

"I reef her back on her haunches beside the verandah just in front of this Carruthers mob and they're on their feet shoving back chairs before they've swallowed their last mouthful of grog.

"Well, I jam my heels into Gay Girl's flanks then, and she's into it, squealing like a pig. She tries to brush me off against a tree—she's like that, a dirty bucker. I drag her round, flapping me hat against her ribs and she bounds sideways on to the verandah. She's a twisting bucker and every time she spins she knocks over a chair or a table. There's glasses of grog flying everywhere, and blokes jumping up, and women screaming, and some of the blokes jump between me and the women with faces on them like they was heroes, and women hang on to 'em, and the boat's going down, and throw out the lifebelts, and kiss me goodbye, and God Save the King, and all that sort of thing. Hell! you never saw the like."

When father reached this stage of the story he began laughing and didn't stop till he had wiped his eyes with his handkerchief.

"Aw, hell!" he said, taking a breath, then concluded, "Well, before I quieten her, I knock Sir Frederick Salisbury, or whatever his name is, head over turkey into a clump of peacocks."

"Did all this happen, dad?" I asked him once. "Is it true?"

"Hell, yes . . . Well, wait a minute . . ." He screwed up his face and rubbed his chin with his hand. "Well, no, son, I suppose it isn't," he decided. "Something like that happened but after you tell it a few times you keep on making it better and funnier, see. I'm not telling lies. I'm telling a funny story. It's good to make people laugh. There's a hell of a lot of other things making them sad."

"Is it like that about the deer?" I asked him.

"Yes," he said. "It is, a bit. I rode him but that's all."

Why Mr. Carruthers protested against father was because father rode his deer.

"There he was going round and round and round," he told me. "Poor beggar . . . I was up there with some of the boys and I stood on the fence and as he passed beneath me I jumped on to his back. They reckon I wasn't game, of course." He paused, looking ahead of him and stroking his chin, a faint smile on his face, then added, "Hell!" in a tone that suggested a terrific reaction from the deer.

He would never tell me much about this escapade, which he seemed to regard as childish. All he would say when I asked "Did he go?" was "Did he what!"

But I asked Peter Finlay about it, thinking that father's reluctance to talk about it must have meant he was thrown.

"Did the deer toss father?" I asked Peter.

"No," he said, "your father tossed the deer."

Later, someone told me the deer broke a horn on father and this was what annoyed Mr. Carruthers who saved the deer's horns and put them over his mantelpiece.

After Mr. Carruthers died, Mrs. Carruthers sent the deer away, but, when I was old enough to go sneaking through the estate, you could still see the deep track it had made walking round and round.

It was because of these things and because of the awe in which everyone in Turalla, except father, held Mrs. Carruthers that I looked at this box on the bed before me almost reverently, valuing it far more than any other gift I had received. It was valuable not because it could entertain me—a candlebox on wheels would have pleased me better—but because it was evidence that Mrs. Carruthers was aware of my existence and that she thought me important enough for her to buy me a present.

No other person in all Turalla had ever had a gift from Mrs. Carruthers—only me. And she had a rubber-tyred Abbot buggy and a pair of grey horses and peacocks and millions of pounds.

"Mum," I said looking up at her, my hands still clasped round the box, "when Mrs. Carruthers handed Mary the present, did Mary touch her?"

6

Next morning I was not given any breakfast but I did not feel very hungry. I was restless and excited and had moments of fear during which I wanted mother.

At half past ten Nurse Conrad wheeled a trolley, resembling a narrow table on wheels, beside my bed and said, "Come on. Sit up now. I'm going to take you for a ride."

She pulled back my blankets.

"I'll get on," I said. "I'll get on it."

"No, I'll lift you," she said. "Don't you like me putting my arms around you?"

I looked quickly at Angus and then at Mick to see if they had heard.

"Go on," Mick called out. "She's the prettiest bell wether you're ever likely to meet. Give her a go."

She lifted me in her arms and held me a moment, smiling down at me, "I'm not a bell wether, am I?"

"No," I replied, not understanding that a bell wether was the Judas sheep of the slaughter yards trained to lead those about to be slaughtered into the killing pen.

She laid me on the cold, flat top of the trolley and covered me with a blanket.

"Away we go!" she said gaily.

"Keep your pecker up," encouraged Angus. "You'll be back with us soon."

"Yes, he's going to wake up in his own warm bed," said Nurse Conrad.

"Good luck to you!" called Mick.

The drunk raised himself on an elbow and said hoarsely to me as we passed his bed, "Thanks for the eggs, mate." Then he added more strongly, "Good on ya!"

Nurse Conrad wheeled me down a long corridor and through glass doors into the theatre in the centre of which stood a high table with thin, white legs.

Sister Cooper and a nurse were standing near a bench upon which steel instruments lay on a white cloth.

"Well, here you are!" exclaimed the sister walking over to me and stroking my head.

I looked into her eyes, seeking assurance there.

"Feeling frightened?" she asked.

"Yes."

"You silly boy. There's nothing to be frightened of. In a minute you'll go to sleep and after a little while you'll wake up in your bed again."

I could not understand how this was possible. I was certain I would wake up from any sleep if the nurses tried to move me. I wondered whether they were just saying this to fool me and that, instead of waking up in my bed, something painful was going to happen to me. But I believed Nurse Conrad.

"I'm not frightened," I said to the sister.

"I know you're not," she said confidentially as she lifted me on to the table and placed a low pillow beneath my head. "Now don't move or you'll roll off."

Dr. Robertson entered briskly and stood smiling down at me as he massaged his fingers.

" 'Sh! Sh! Go out black cat', so that's the song you sing, is it?"

He patted me and turned away.

"Abbot buggies and black cats, eh!" he murmured as a nurse came forward and helped him into a white gown. "Abbot buggies and black cats! Well! Well!"

Dr. Clarke, a grey-haired man with a tight-lipped mouth, walked in.

"The Council hasn't filled in that hole near the gate yet," he said, turning to face a nurse holding his white gown up in front of her ready for him to slip it on. "I don't know . . . Can you rely on any man's word these days? This gown seems too big . . . No, it's mine all right."

I looked at the white ceiling and thought of the puddle near our gate that always came after rain; I could jump it easily but Mary couldn't. I could jump any puddle.

Dr. Clarke had moved round to my head where he stood holding a hollowed, white pad like a shell, above my nose.

At a sign from Dr. Robertson he saturated the pad with liquid he poured from a little blue bottle and I gasped as I drew a laden breath. I jerked my head from side to side but he followed my nose with the pad and I saw coloured lights, then clouds came and I floated away upon them.

I did not wake up in my bed as Sister Cooper and Nurse Conrad had promised. I fought through haze and a swinging world without comprehending where I was until suddenly, in a moment of clarity, I saw the ceiling of the theatre again. Then, after a little while, I could see the sister's face. She was saying something to me but I could not hear her. But, in a moment I could, and she was saying, "Wake up."

After I had lain quietly for a while I remembered everything and I suddenly felt cheated.

"I'm not in bed like you said," I muttered.

"No, you woke up before we got you there," she explained, then added, "You mustn't move even the tiniest bit. The plaster on your leg is still wet."

I became conscious of my heavy leg and the stone-like clasp of the plaster encircling my hips and waist.

"Lie still now," she said. "I'm going out for a minute. Watch him, nurse," she said to Nurse Conrad who was putting instruments away into glass cases.

Nurse Conrad came over to me. "How's my boy now?" she asked.

Her face was beautiful to me. I loved her plump cheeks, flushed like apples, and her twinkling little eyes tucked away beneath thick, dark brows and long lashes. I wanted her to stop with me and not go away and I wanted to give her a horse and gig. But I felt sick and I was shy and couldn't tell her these things.

"Don't move, will you?" she cautioned me.

"I think I might have moved my toes a bit," I said.

The repeated warnings not to move made me want to move just to see what would happen. I felt that once I knew I could move I would be satisfied and stop.

"You mustn't even move your toes," she said.

"I won't again," I told her.

I was kept on the operating table until lunch time, then wheeled carefully to my bed where a steel framework held the blankets high above my legs and prevented me from seeing Mick across the ward.

It was visiting day and relatives and friends of the patients began to arrive. They strode down the ward laden with parcels, looking neither to the right nor the left, acutely conscious of the sick people each side of them as they kept their gaze on the patient they were visiting. The patients were self-conscious as they awaited the visitors approaching them. They looked away from them, pretending not to notice them until they stood beside their bed.

Those patients who had no friends or relatives to visit them did not lack for visitors. A Salvation Army lass or a Minister or a Priest would stop and talk to them—and then, there was always Miss Forbes.

Miss Forbes came each visiting day laden with flowers and tracts and bedsocks. She must have been seventy years old. She walked stiffly, helped by a stick, and she would tap this stick against the end of the bed of those who ignored her and say, "Well, young man, I hope you're doing what the doctor tells you. That is the way to get well, you know. Now, here are some currant cakes for you. If you chew them well they won't give you indigestion. Always chew your food well."

She always gave me a humbug lolly.

"They clear the chest," she said.

She stopped at the foot of my bed as usual and said gently, "So you have been under an operation today, have you? Well, the doctors know what they're doing and I'm sure it's all for the best. So never mind, there's a good boy. Never mind, there's a good boy."

My leg was aching and I was lonely. I began to cry.

She was concerned and came quickly round to the side of my bed and stood there awkwardly, anxious to comfort me but uncertain what she should do.

"God will help you to bear your suffering," she said earnestly. "Here! I have some messages here."

She took some tracts from her handbag and handed me one.

"You read that; there's a good boy."

51

She touched my hand and walked self-consciously away, but she looked back at me several times, her face troubled.

I looked at the tract in my hand, feeling it might contain some magic, some sign from God, some inspired message that would enable me to get up and walk like Lazarus.

The tract was headed, "Why Are Ye Troubled?" and it began, "If living a stranger to God, you may well be troubled. The thought of death and judgment to come may well give you trouble. If this is your condition, God grant that your trouble may be greater and greater, until you find rest in Jesus."

I didn't understand it. I put it on my locker and continued crying softly.

"How're you feeling now, Alan?" asked Angus.

"I feel heavy," I said. After a while I told him, "My leg is aching."

"It will soon stop," he said to comfort me.

But it didn't stop.

When lying on the operating table, the plaster around my right leg and around my waist still moist and soft, I must have lifted my big toe in some brief spasm but lacked the strength in my paralysed muscles to force it down again to its natural position. Some movement of my hip, too, had lifted the inside plaster bandage, setting it in a ridge that pressed like a blunt knife against my hip bone. Gradually over the next two weeks this ridge ground its way into my flesh till it touched the bone itself.

The pain from my lifted toe was unceasing but I got some relief from my torn hip when I lay still with my body twisted a little. Even in the short intervals of sleep that came to me between the waiting periods of pain, I had dreams in which I moved through other worlds of suffering.

Dr. Robertson looked frowningly down at me as he pondered on my descriptions of my pains.

"Are you sure it is your toe that is paining you?"

"Yes. All the while," I told him. "It never stops."

"It must be his knee," he said to the matron. "He probably imagines it is his toe. And this pain in your hip . . ." He turned to me, "Does your hip ache all the time too?"

"It hurts when I move. It doesn't hurt when I lie still."

He pushed against the plaster above my hip.

"Does that hurt?"

"Oo!" I exclaimed, trying to move away from him. "Oo, yes!"

"Hm!" he muttered.

A week after the operation, an angry defiance that had enabled me to bear the pain gave way to despair, and the fear I had of being thought a baby did not help me any more. I began to cry more often. I cried silently, gazing open-eyed through my tears at the high, white ceiling above me. I wished I was dead, seeing in death not a frightening absence of life, but a sleeping without pain.

I began repeating over and over again in my mind in a jerky rhythm, "I wish I were dead, I wish I were dead, I wish I were dead."

I found, after a few days, that by jerking my head from side to side to the rhythm of the repeated words, I achieved a mental distraction that brought relief from the pain. By keeping my eyes open as I flung my head from side to side on the pillow, the white ceiling quickly became blurred and the bed upon which I lay rose on wings from the floor.

Beyond this first dizzy state was a nebulous, clouded place wherein I swung in mighty curves through darkness and light free from pain but gripped by nausea.

Here I remained until the will to continue tossing my head was lost to me and I slowly returned, moving towards formless shadows that shimmered and swayed and then materialised into the beds and windows and walls of the ward.

I usually sought this relief at night but sometimes, if the pain was bad, I did it in the daytime when the nurses were out of the ward.

Angus must have noticed me jerking my head from side to side for one day he asked quickly, just as I had begun moving my head, "What d'you do that for, Alan?"

"Nothing," I said.

"Come on, now," he said. "We're mates. What makes you jerk your head? Are you in pain?"

"It stops the pain."

"Oh!" he said. "Is that it! How does it stop the pain?"

"I don't feel it. I get giddy an' that," I explained.

He did not say anything but later I heard him telling Nurse Conrad that something had better be done about it.

53

"He's game," he said. "He wouldn't do that unless he was crook."

That night the sister gave me the needle and I slept without waking but next day the pain continued and I was given doses of A.P.C. and told to lie quietly and go to sleep.

I waited till the nurse had left the ward and then began rocking my head again. But she had expected it and was watching me through the glass door.

Her name was Nurse Freeborn and no one liked her. She was strict and efficient and only did what she had to do.

"I'm not a servant," she said to a patient who asked her to hand me a magazine. Sometimes she would say, "Can't you see I'm on my rounds?" when asked to do something that would hinder her for a moment.

She came back swiftly.

"You naughty boy," she said sharply. "Stop doing that at once. If ever you shake your head like that again I'll tell the doctor and he'll give it to you. You mustn't do that. Now you lie quietly. I'll be watching you."

She strode away, her lips compressed, but looked back at me once more before she passed through the doorway.

"Remember, now, if I catch you shaking your head again, look out."

Angus scowled at the doorway.

"Did you hear that?" he said to Mick. "Fancy her being a nurse. Hell . . ."

"Her!" Mick gestured contemptuously. "She told me I was suffering from Imaginitis. I'll give her Imaginitis. Next time she chips me I'll tell her off, you see if I don't. Take no notice of her, Alan," he called to me.

A local infection began to develop in my hip where the plaster had cut into the flesh, and in the next few days it reached the stage where I suddenly felt a boil had broken high up somewhere on my leg. The dull ache of my toe had been hard to stand that day and now this burning sensation in my hip . . . I began sobbing in a hopeless, tired manner then I noticed Angus watching me with a troubled expression. I raised myself on my elbow and looked at him in a way that must have revealed my desperation for his face suddenly showed concern.

"Mr. McDonald," I said, my voice trembling. "I'm sick of pain. I want it stopped. I think I'm busted."

He slowly closed the book he was reading and sat up looking towards the ward door.

"Where's the bloody nurses?" he called out to Mick in a savage voice. "You can walk. Go out and get them. Send Daddy for them. He'll do. This kid's had enough. I'd like to know what his old man'd say if he was here. Hop out and tell one of the nurses I want her, Daddy. Hurry up."

In a little while a nurse came in and looked enquiringly at Angus.

"What's the matter?"

He nodded towards me. "Have a look at him. He's crook."

She raised my blankets and, seeing the sheet, she lowered them again without speaking and hurried away.

I remember being surrounded by the doctor, the matron, and the nurses and I remember the doctor sawing and hacking the plaster from my leg, but I was burning hot and giddy and I didn't remember father or mother coming. I remember father bringing me some parrot feathers but that was a week later.

7

WHEN I again became conscious of the ward and its inmates there was a stranger in Angus's bed. Both Angus and Mick had been discharged the week I had been ill. Angus had left me three eggs and a half jar of pickles and Mick had given Nurse Conrad a jam tin full of bush honey to give to me "When I came good again."

I missed them. The ward seemed to have changed. The men who now lay in the white beds were too ill or too subdued by their unfamiliar surroundings to sing out to each other and they had not yet learned to share their eggs.

Daddy was gloomier than ever.

"This place is not what it used to be," he told me. "I can remember arguments going on in this ward—you never heard the like. Clever blokes, too, some of 'em. Just take a look at this mob. You wouldn't give two bob for the lot. They come in here with guts ache then roll their eyes like they got consumption. They won't listen to a bloke's troubles; all they think of is their pains and aches. If I wasn't gonner die any tick o' the clock I'd ask the matron to let me go. An' she's a beautiful woman, mind you!"

The man in Angus's bed was very tall and when Nurse Conrad tucked in his blankets just after he had arrived, she exclaimed, "My! You are a big man!"

He was pleased. He smiled self-consciously and looked round the ward to see if we had all heard, then he settled deeper into the bed, stretching his long legs so that his toes thrust the blankets through the bars at the foot and clasping his hands behind his head.

"Can you ride?" I asked him, impressed by his size.

He looked at me quickly, then, seeing I was a child, he ignored the question and continued his survey of the ward. I wondered whether he thought I was cheeky, then, feeling indignant, I convinced myself I didn't care what he thought.

But he always spoke to Nurse Conrad.

"You're all right," he'd say to her.

He didn't seem able to say much else when she waited for him to continue. Sometimes he would try to grab her hand when she was taking his pulse and when she jerked it away he'd say, "You're all right."

She always had to be careful when standing near his bed or he'd slap her on the back and say, "You're all right."

"Don't do that again," she said sharply to him once.

"You're all right," he said.

"And following up with that remark doesn't smooth it over either," she said looking at him with some cold knowledge in her eyes.

I couldn't make him out. He never said "You're all right" to anyone else.

One day he spent the afternoon frowning and writing on a sheet of paper and that night, when she was removing his quilt, he said, "I've written a piece of poetry about you."

She looked surprised, then suspicious.

"Do you write poetry?" she asked pausing in her work and looking at him.

"Yes," he said. "It comes natural to me. I can write poetry about anything."

He gave her the sheet of paper and she read the poem, a pleased expression growing on her face.

"That's real good," she said. "It is. It's real good. Where did you learn to write poetry?"

She turned the paper over and looked at the back then read the poem a second time.

"Can I keep this? It's real good."

"That's nothing." He waved a deprecating hand. "I'll write you another tomorrow. Keep that. I can turn 'em out any time. I don't have to think. It's natural to me."

Nurse Conrad turned to fix my bed, placing the sheet of paper on my locker while she folded the quilt.

"You can read it," she said, noticing me glancing towards it. She handed it to me and I read it slowly and laboriously.

NURSE CONRAD

Nurse Conrad comes and makes our beds,
And wonders why we get it into our heads
That she is the nicest nurse in the hospital,
And I'm telling you this is gospel,
Because no other nurse is as pretty as her,
Or half as nice to the patients who suffer.
She always comes at your call,
And is loved by everyone, one and all.

When I finished reading it I didn't know what to say. I liked what it said about Nurse Conrad but I didn't like him saying it. I thought it must be good because it was poetry and they made you read poetry at school and our teacher was always saying how good poetry was.

"It's good," I said wistfully.

I wished I had written it. A horse and gig seemed nothing beside a man who could write poetry.

I felt tired and wished I was home where no one wrote poetry and where I could jump on Kate and go trotting round the yard while father called out, "Sit up straight now . . . Keep your hands down . . . Head up . . . Get the feel of her mouth . . . Push your legs forward. Right. That's good. Straighter still . . . Good on you."

If Nurse Conrad could only see me on Kate.

8

My leg from the knee to the ankle was now in a splint and my foot and waist were not confined in plaster. The pain had gone and I didn't wish I were dead any more.

"The bone is slow in knitting," I heard Dr. Robertson tell the matron. "The circulation is poor in that leg."

One day he said to the matron, "He's pale . . . No sunshine . . . Put him in a wheelchair each day and let him sit in the sun. How would you like to ride round in a wheelchair?" he asked me.

I could not answer him.

That afternoon the sister pushed a wheelchair beside my bed. She laughed as she saw the expression upon my face.

"You'll be able to race Daddy now," she said. "Come on; sit up till I get my arm round you."

She lifted me into the chair, lowering my legs gently till they rested against the woven cane back of the lower framework. My feet could not reach the wooden support that projected like a shelf at the bottom of the leg-rest. My legs dangled uselessly, the feet pointing downwards.

I looked down at the support, feeling disappointed that my legs were too short to reach it. I could see myself chair-racing under a great handicap but I had no doubt father would rig up a rest that I could reach, and my arms were strong.

I was proud of my arms. I grasped the wooden rails that circled the spokes but I felt giddy and let the sister push me through the ward door, down the corridor and out into the bright world.

As we passed through the door leading to the garden, the fresh, open air and the sunshine poured itself over me in one immense torrent. I rose to meet it, sitting upright in my chair,

C

facing the blue and the sparkle and the gentle push of the air against my face, like a diver rising from the sea.

For three months I had not seen a cloud or felt the sun upon me. Now they were returned to me, newly created, perfected, radiant with qualities they never possessed before.

The sister left me in the sunshine near some sheoak trees and though there was no wind I could hear them whispering together as father said they always do.

I wondered what had happened to things while I had been away, what had changed them so. I watched a dog trotting along the street on the other side of the high picket fence. I had never seen such a wonderful dog, so pattable, so full of possibilities. A grey thrush called and its note was a gift to me. I looked down at the gravel upon which my chair rested. Each grain had colour and they lay there in their millions, tossed into strange little hills and hollows. Some had escaped into the grass which skirted the pathway and the grass stems leant over them in lovely curves of tenderness.

I could hear the shouts of children at play and the clip-clop of a trotting horse. A dog barked and away out over the resting houses there came the whistle of a train.

The foliage of the sheoaks drooped like coarse hair and through it I could see the sky. The leaves of the gum trees glittered, throwing off diamonds of sunshine that hurt my eyes, unprepared for such brightness.

I hung my head and closed my eyes and the sun wrapped itself round me like arms.

After a while I raised my head and began to experiment with the chair, grasping the rails like Daddy and trying to turn the wheels, but the gravel was too deep and the pathway was flanked with stones.

I became interested in seeing how far I could spit. I knew a boy who could spit across a road but he had a front tooth out. I felt my teeth but none of them were loose.

I studied the sheoaks and decided I could climb them all except one and it wasn't worth climbing.

After a while a boy came walking up the street. He clattered a stick along the pickets as he walked and he was followed by a brown dog. I knew the boy. His name was George and his mother brought him each visiting day to the hospital. He often gave me things—comics, cigarette cards, and sometimes lollies.

I liked him because he was a good rabbiter and had a ferret. He was kind, too.

"There's lots of things I'd give you," he told me once, "but I'm not let."

His dog's name was Snipe and this dog was so small he could go down burrows but he could fight anything so long as he had a fair go, George told me.

"If you want to be a good rabbiter you've got to have a good dog," was one of George's convictions.

I agreed with this but thought a greyhound was good to have if your mother would let you keep it.

This fitted in with George's ideas on greyhounds. He told me darkly that "Women don't like greyhounds."

This was exactly what I thought.

I regarded George as being very clever and I told mother about him.

"He's a good boy," mother said.

I was a bit doubtful about this and hoped he wasn't too good.

"I don't like a siss, do you?" I asked him later. It was a searching question.

"Hell, no!" he said.

It was a satisfactory answer and I concluded that he wasn't as good as mother thought.

The sight of him coming along the street filled me with joy.

"How's it goin', George?" I yelled.

"Not bad," he said, "but mum said I gotta come straight home."

"Aw!" I exclaimed, disappointed.

"I gotta bag of lollies here," he informed me in the tone of one mentioning a commonplace.

"What sort?"

"London Mixture."

"They're the best, I reckon. Are there any of those round ones—you know—with hundreds and thousands stuck on 'em?"

"No," said George, "I ate 'em."

"Aw! did you!" I murmured, suddenly depressed.

"Come over to the fence and I'll give you what's left," George urged me. "I don't want 'em. We got hundreds at home."

It was a request I would not have thought of refusing but after an automatic but futile struggle I told him, "I can't walk yet. They're still curing me. I'd do it if I didn't have a splint on but I've got a splint on."

"Well, I'll pitch 'em over," announced George.

"Good on ya, George!"

George stepped back on to the roadway to take a run at it. I watched him approvingly. If ever there was a boy who demonstrated by text-book preliminaries that he was a perfect thrower, that boy was George.

He eyed the distance, loosened his shoulders . . .

"Well, here she comes!" he cried.

He began his run with a graceful skip—the touch of a perfectionist—took three long strides and threw.

Any girl could have thrown better.

"I slipped," George explained in a tone of exasperation. "Me darn foot slipped."

I didn't see George slip but there was no doubt he must have slipped and slipped badly.

I looked at the bag of lollies lying some eight yards away from me on the grass and said, "Listen! How about you going round to the gate and coming in and getting them?"

"I can't," explained George. "Mum's waiting for the suet to cook. She said I gotta come straight home. Leave them there and I'll get them for you tomorrow. No one will touch 'em. By hell I must go!"

"All right," I said resignedly, "that'll have to do."

"Well, I'm off," called George. "See you tomorrow. Hurroo."

"Hurroo, George," I called abstractedly. I was looking at the lollies and trying to work out some way of getting them.

Eating a lolly was, to me, a delightful experience. When father paid his monthly bill at the store he always took me with him and after the storekeeper had handed father the receipt, he would say to me, "Well, my little man, what would you like? I know—lollies. Well, let's see what we can do."

He would twist a piece of white paper into a cone and fill it with boiled lollies and give it to me and I would say, "Thank you, Mr. Simmons."

I always kept the lollies for a while before I looked at them or ate them. The hard feel of them beneath the paper, each little bump representing a lolly, the weight of them in my hand, these were so full of suggestion I wanted to enjoy them first. Besides I always divided them with Mary when I got home.

Boiled lollies were good but I was allowed, as with those given to me by the storekeeper, to keep on eating them till the bag was finished. This lowered their value a little, suggesting, as it did, that they were not valued by adults.

There were lollies so expensive I was only allowed a taste. Once father bought a thrupenny cake of milk chocolate and mother gave Mary and me a square each. The taste of that milk chocolate dissolving on my tongue was delightful and I often recalled it as one would a significant event. "I'd sooner milk chocolate than chops any day," I told mother as she bent over the wire griller.

"Some day I'll buy you a cake of it," she told me.

There were times when a man gave me a penny for holding his horse and when this happened I would run to the baker's shop, where lollies were sold, and stand gazing into the window at the display of Rum-rum-go-goes, Milk Poles, Silver Sticks, Cough Sticks, Sherbet Suckers, Licorice Straps, Aniseed Balls and Snowballs. I did not notice the few dying blowflies lying on their backs between the packets and straps and sticks, feebly moving their legs and sometimes buzzing. I only saw the lollies. I would stand there a long time quite unable to make up my mind what to buy.

On those rare occasions when some squatter gave me thrupence for the same job, I was immediately surrounded by my school mates who passed on the news from boy to boy with shrill cries, "Alan's got thrupence."

Then came the important question, "Are you going to spend it all at once or keep some for tomorrow?"

On the answer to this depended the extent to which each boy would share in my purchases and they awaited the decision with restraint.

My answer, in the form of an announcement, was always the same, "I'm going to spend the lot."

It was a decision that invariably brought forth yells of approval then scuffles to decide who would walk each side of me and behind me and in front of me.

"I'm your mate, Alan . . . You know me, Alan . . . I gave ya the core of me apple yesterdee . . . I got here first . . . Let go a me . . . I always been mates with Alan, haven't I Alan?"

It was recognised in our school that, so long as a boy was clutching you, he had some claim on you or, at least, was entitled to a consideration of any demands he made. I walked in the centre of a little, compact group, each boy attached to me by a resolute hand. I clutched the thrupence.

We came to a halt in front of the window and now I was deluged with advice.

"Remember, ya get eight aniseed balls for a penny, Alan . . . How many of us are here, Sam? There's eight here, Alan . . . Licorice straps go the furthest of any lolly . . . Sherbet suckers are beaut . . . You can make drinks out of sherbet suckers . . . Let go a me . . . I was beside him first . . . Fancy, thrupence! You can have a lend of me shanghai any time you want it, Alan."

I looked at the bag of lollies on the grass. The thought that it would be impossible for me to get them of my own accord was an alternative I did not consider for a moment. Those lollies were mine. They were given to me. Blow my legs! I would get them.

The chair was standing on the edge of the pathway that skirted the grassy plot on which the lollies were lying. I seized its arm-rests and began to rock it from side to side till it hung poised on a slanting wheel at the end of each sway; then I gave an extra lift and it crashed to its side, flinging me face downwards on the grass. My splinted leg struck the stone border of the pathway and the sudden pain made me mutter angrily and pull some grass out by the roots. The pale roots, holding in their clasp a lump of granulated soil, seemed, in some strange way, a comforting thing. In a moment I began to drag myself towards the lollies, leaving behind me as I progressed, some pillows, a rug, a comic. . . .

When I reached the paper bag I grasped it in my hand and smiled.

Once, when I had climbed a tree to put a pulley rope over a limb for father, he called out delightedly from below, "You did it. By hell, you did it!"

I did it, I thought, and I opened the bag, and after a moment's pleased inspection, extracted a conversation lolly upon which I read the words, "I love you."

I sucked it appreciatively, taking it out of my mouth every few moments to see if I could still read the words. They faded, became a line of meaningless depressions, then vanished. I held a little pink disc in my hand. I lay on my back looking through the branches of a sheoak and crushed the lolly between my teeth.

I felt very happy.

9

THE consternation that seized the nurses who found me lying on the grass surprised me. I could not understand the summoning of the matron, the gathering round my bed and the mixture of concern and anger that marked their interrogation.

I kept repeating, "I tipped myself over to get the lollies," and when the matron insisted on me answering, "But why? Why didn't you call a nurse?" I answered, "I wanted to get them by myself."

"I can't understand you," she complained.

I wondered why she couldn't. I knew father would. When I told him, he said, "Couldn't you have sort of climbed out of the chair without tipping it over?"

"No," I said, "I couldn't use my legs, see."

"I see," he said, then added, "Well, you got them anyway. I wouldn't have called a nurse either. She would have got them all right but then it would have been different."

"It would have been different," I said, liking him more than ever.

"But don't hurt yourself next time," he warned me. "Be careful. Don't tip yourself out for lollies again. They're not worth it. Tip yourself out for big things—like a fire or something. I'd have bought you some lollies but I'm not holding too good this week."

"I don't want any this week," I said to comfort him.

For the next few weeks I was watched very carefully when I sat in the wheelchair on the verandah; then one day the doctor arrived carrying a pair of crutches.

"Here are your front legs," he told me. "Do you think you could walk on these? Come on and we'll try."

"Are they really and truly mine?" I asked him.

"Yes," he said, "really and truly . . ."

I was sitting in the wheelchair out in the garden and he pushed it on to the grass under the sheoak trees.

"This is a good place. We'll try here."

The matron and some of the nurses had come out to see me attempt my first walk on crutches and they gathered round while the doctor placed his hands beneath my arms and lifted me up from the chair, holding me erect in front of him.

The matron, to whom he had handed the crutches, placed them beneath my armpits and then he lowered me till I was resting my weight on the armpit rests.

"Are you right?" he asked.

"No," I said, suddenly unsure of myself. "I'm not right yet. I'll be right in a minute."

"Take it easy," he instructed me. "Don't try and walk yet. Just stand. I'm holding you. You can't fall."

My right leg, the one I called my "bad" leg, was completely paralysed and swung uselessly from the hip, a thing of skin and bone, scarred and deformed. I called my left leg my "good" leg. It was only partially paralysed and could bear my weight. For weeks I had been testing it while sitting on the edge of my bed.

The curvature of my spine gave me a decided lean to the left but resting on the crutches pulled it temporarily straight, and my body lengthened so that, standing, I appeared taller than when sitting down.

My stomach muscles were partially paralysed but my chest and arms were unaffected. In the years that were to follow I came to regard my legs as not worth much consideration. They angered me, though sometimes they seemed to live a sad life of their own apart from me and I felt sorry for them. My arms and chest were my pride and they were to develop out of all proportion to the rest of my body.

I stood there uncertainly for a moment looking ahead towards where, a few yards away, a bare patch of ground was worn in the grass.

I will get there, I thought, and waited, not knowing exactly what muscles to call upon, conscious that the crutches beneath my armpits were hurting me and that I must move them forward and take my weight for a moment on my good leg if I wanted to walk.

The doctor had taken his hands away but he held them apart one each side of me, ready to grab me should I fall.

I lifted the crutches and swung them heavily forward, my shoulders jerking upwards to the sudden jar as my weight came down on the armpit rests once more. I swung my legs forward, my right leg dragging in the dirt like a broken wing. I paused, breathing deeply and looking at the bare patch of earth ahead of me.

"Good!" exclaimed the doctor as I made this first step. "Now again."

I went through the same movements again, then three times more till at last I stood achingly upon the patch of earth. I had walked.

"That will do for today," said the doctor. "Back into your chair. You can have another try tomorrow."

In a few weeks I could walk round the garden and though I had fallen a few times I had acquired confidence and was beginning to practise leaping from the verandah, seeing how far I could jump from a line scraped on the path.

When I was told I was going home and that mother was calling for me next day I was not as excited as I had thought I would be. The hospital had gradually taken the form of a permanent background to my thoughts and activities. My life had become ordered and I felt, in an unexpressed way, that in leaving the hospital I would lose the security I had acquired there. I was a little afraid of going and yet I was eager to see where the street that passed the hospital led to, what was going on down there beyond the rise where shunting trains puffed and trucks banged together and cabs carrying people with bags came and went. And I wanted to see dad breaking in horses again.

When mother arrived I was dressed and sitting on the edge of my bed looking at the empty wheelchair I would not be able to ride in again. Father didn't have enough money to buy a wheelchair but he had made a long, three-wheeled vehicle out of an old perambulator and mother was wheeling this.

68

She was to take me down the street where father had left a waggonette in the pub yard while he got a pair of horses shod.

When Nurse Conrad kissed me goodbye, I wanted to cry but I didn't and I gave her all the eggs I had left and some *War Cries* and the parrot feathers father had brought me. I had nothing else to give her but she said that was enough.

The matron patted my head and told mother I was a brave little fellow and that, in one way, it was fortunate I was crippled so young in that I would now have no difficulty in adjusting myself to a lifetime on crutches.

"Children are so adaptable," she assured mother.

Mother, looking at me, seemed possessed by some deep sadness when the matron said this, and she did not reply to her which I thought was rude of mother.

The nurses waved to me and Daddy shook my hand and said I'd never see him again. He'd be gone any tick o' the clock now.

Mother had wrapped me in a rug and I lay in the pram clutching a little lion made of clay that Nurse Conrad had given me.

She wheeled me on to the street and pushed me along the pathway and over the rise. There weren't the wonderful things I thought there would be over this rise. The houses were no different from other houses and the railway station was just a shed.

She pushed me over a kerb and through a gutter then up again, but somehow one of the wheels went over the edge of the paving and the pram tipped over and I fell into the gutter.

Mother's efforts to raise the pram from where it lay half on top of me, and her anxious demands to know whether I was hurt were lost to me. I was too busy searching for my clay lion and there he was, sure enough, underneath the rug with his head broken off as I had expected.

A man had dashed forward in answer to mother's call.

"Could you help me lift my little boy back?" she asked him.

"What's wrong?" exclaimed the man seizing the pram and lifting it with a quick heave. "What's wrong with the kid?"

"I tipped him over. Be careful! Don't hurt him; he's lame!"

This last exclamation of mother's shocked me into a sudden awareness of my part in this unnecessary excitement. The word "lame" was associated in my mind with limping horses and suggested complete uselessness.

I raised myself on my elbow in the gutter, looking at mother with an expression of astonishment.

"Lame, mum?" I exclaimed with some force. "What did you say I was lame for?"

10

THE word "crippled", to me, suggested a condition that
could be applied to some people, but not to myself. But,
since I so often heard people refer to me as crippled, I was
forced to concede that I must fit this description, yet retained
a conviction that though being crippled was obviously a dis-
tressing state for some people, with me it didn't matter.

The crippled child is not conscious of the handicap implied
by his useless legs. They are often inconvenient or annoying
but he is confident that they will never prevent him doing what
he wants to do or being whatever he wishes to be. If he con-
siders them a handicap it is because he has been told they are.

Children make no distinction between the one who is lame
and the one who has the full use of his limbs. They will ask a
boy on crutches to run here or there for them and complain
when he is slow.

In childhood a useless leg does not bring with it a sense of
shame; it is only when one learns to interpret the glance of
people unable to hide their feelings that one experiences a desire
to avoid them. And, strangely enough, this unshielded glance
of distaste only comes from those who have weak bodies, who
carry with them a consciousness of some physical inferiority;
it never comes from those who are strong and healthy. Strong
and healthy people do not shrink from the cripple; his state
is so remote from them. It is those under the threat of helplessness who quail when confronted with it in another.

A useless leg, a twisted limb, is freely discussed by children.
"Come an' see Alan's funny leg. He can put it over his head."
"How did you get your sore leg?"

The pained mother, hearing her son announce bluntly,
"Here's Alan, mum. His leg is all crooked," hastens to stop

him saying more, forgetting she is facing two happy little boys, her son proud of his exhibit, Alan happy to be able to provide it.

A crippled limb often adds to the importance of its owner and he is sometimes privileged because of it.

In circus games I accepted the role of donkey—"because you have four legs"—with a great display of kicking and bucking, enjoying being able to do this and seeing my four legs as being most desirable.

Children's sense of humour is not restricted by adult ideas of good taste and tact. They often laughed at the spectacle of me on crutches and shouted with merriment when I fell over. I joined in their laughter, gripped by some sense of absurdity that made a stumble on crutches an hilarious thing.

When high paling fences had to be negotiated I was often pushed over and a collapse of those taking my weight was regarded as extremely funny, not only by those helping me but by myself too.

I was happy. I had no pain and could walk. But the grown-up people who visited our home when I returned did not expect me to be happy. They called my happiness "courage". Most grown-up people talk frankly about children in front of them, as if children are incapable of understanding references to themselves.

"He's a happy kid despite his affliction, Mrs. Marshall," they would say as if surprised that this were so.

Why shouldn't I be happy? I thought. The suggestion that I should be other than happy troubled me in that it implied the presence in my life of some disaster I did not recognise but which would catch up on me some day. I wondered what it was and at last concluded they imagined my leg pained me.

"My leg doesn't hurt," I'd say brightly to those who expressed surprised approval of my smiling face. "Look!" and I would lift my bad leg with my hands and place it over my head.

This made some people shudder and my puzzlement increased. My legs were so familiar to me that I viewed them as one would normal limbs and not as objects that raised a minor revulsion.

Those parents who told their children to be gentle with me or who felt they should correct what they considered an unfeeling attitude in their children, only succeeded in confusing them. Some children, subject to the counselling of parents anxious to "make things easier" for me, would sometimes protest against the treatment I was getting from their mates.

"Don't bump him; you'll hurt his leg."

But I wanted to be bumped and though I was not naturally aggressive I developed an aggressiveness to counter what I regarded as unnecessary and humiliating concessions.

Having a normal mind my attitude to life was that of a normal child and my crippled limbs could not alter this attitude. It was when I was treated as someone different from the children with whom I played that my development had to include provisions to meet these influences that would have harnessed my mind to my crippled body.

There is not a state of mind peculiar to crippled children and differing in its attitude to life around them from that of children with sound bodies. Those who stumble on crutches or fall or automatically use their hand to move a paralysed limb are not thinking in terms of frustration and suffering nor are they occupied with the difficulty of getting from one place to another; they are occupied with their object in going there as are all children who run across a paddock or walk up a street.

Suffering because of being crippled is not for you in your childhood; it is reserved for those men and women who look at you.

My first few months at home left me with some awareness of these things but my knowledge was instinctive rather than the result of reasoning.

After the spaciousness of the ward I had to adjust myself to life in a house that suddenly seemed as tiny as a box.

When father lifted the pram from the waggonette and wheeled me into the kitchen I was astonished how it had shrunk. The table with its plush, rose-patterned cover, now seemed to fill the room so completely that there was hardly space for my pram. A strange cat sat licking itself on the brick hearth before the stove.

"Whose cat?" I asked, surprised that this familiar room should contain a cat I had not sponsored.

"It's Blackie's kitten," explained Mary. "You know—she had them before you went to the hospital."

Mary was anxious to tell me everything of importance that had happened since I left.

"And Meg has had five pups and we're calling the little brown one Alan. He's the one dad brought into the hospital to show you."

Mary was excited at my return and had already asked mum if she could take me for walks in my pram. She was older than me and was a devoted, thoughtful person who sat hunched over a book when she wasn't helping mother but who became full of indignant energy when called upon to defend some ill-treated animal, a crusade that took up a lot of her time. Once when a horseman, leaning from his saddle, flogged a lagging and exhausted calf that was unable to keep up with its mother, Mary stood on the top rail of our gate and screamed at him with tears in her voice. When the calf went down, its sides streaked with brown saliva, Mary sped across the track and stood above it with clenched hands. He did not hit it again.

She had dark hair and brown eyes and was always jumping to her feet to get you things. She claimed she was going to be a missionary some day and help the poor Blackfellows. Sometimes she decided she would help the heathen Chinese but she was a little frightened of being massacred.

The *Bulletin* sometimes had pictures of missionaries sitting in pots being cooked by Blackfellows and I had told her it would be better to be massacred than cooked, mainly because I didn't know what massacred meant.

Jane was the eldest in our family and she fed the fowls and kept three lambs a drover had given her when they were too tired to travel. She was tall and walked with her head up. She helped Mrs. Mulvaney, the baker's wife, to look after her babies and she was paid five shillings a week and could buy anything she wanted after she gave mum some.

She had gone into long skirts and put her hair up and she had a pair of tan lace-up boots that went right up almost to her knees. Mrs. Mulvaney thought they were very smart and I thought they were smart, too.

When I walked with her she used to say, "Now, be a little gentleman and raise your cap to Mrs. Mulvaney if we meet her."

74

When I kept thinking about raising my cap I always raised it but I didn't keep thinking about it much.

Jane was at Mrs. Mulvaney's when I arrived home so Mary told me all about the canaries and Pat, the corella, and my pet possum and the king parrot that still hadn't grown a tail. She had fed them every day and hadn't missed once and she had put in two new salmon tins for the canaries' water. The bottom of Pat's cage needed scraping but that was all. The possum still scratched you when you held it but not so much.

I sat there in my pram—mother had hidden my crutches as I was only allowed to use them for an hour each day—and watched mother spread the cloth and set the table for dinner. Mary brought in wood for the stove from the woodbox on the back verandah where the rotting boards hushed the sound of her skipping feet.

Now that I was home the hospital seemed far away, and all that had happened to me there was slipping from reality and remaining in my mind as a story I had experienced. The little things that were now happening around me were re-entering my life with a new vividness, a new magic. The hooks on the brown dresser from which mother was now taking the cups were strangely impressive as if I had never seen the bright curve of them before.

A lamp with a fluted column, a cast-iron base and a pink Edwardian globe stood on the safe beside which my pram was standing. At night it would be taken down and lit and placed in the centre of the table and there would be a circle of bright light beneath it on the cloth.

The safe had sides of perforated zinc and the smell of food came through the holes. Upon the safe there was a sheet of tanglefoot, an oblong of heavy, brown paper covered with a brown sticky substance for catching flies. The sheet was thickly covered with flies, many of them struggling, some buzzing as they beat their wings in a blur of movement. In the summer the flies were thick in the house and you kept waving your hand above your food to keep them away. Father always placed his saucer on top of his cup of tea.

"I don't know," he used to say, "most people can drink their tea after a fly has been in it; I can't."

A big, black kettle with its spout gaping like a striking snake steamed on the stove and above the stove was the mantelpiece girded with a mantel drape of brown baize now dulled by smoke and steam. A tea caddy and a coffee tin with a picture of a bearded Turk upon it stood on the mantelpiece and above the mantelpiece was the picture of the frightened horses. It was good to see this picture again.

Above me on the side wall was the large, framed picture of a boy blowing bubbles that came as a supplement in the Christmas *Pears' Annual*. I raised my head and looked at him with a new interest, my period away from him having quite removed the dislike I had had for his sissy curls and old-fashioned clothes.

A pincushion of blue velvet spiked with pins hung from a nail beneath this picture. It was stuffed with sawdust and you could feel the sawdust when you squeezed it.

Behind the back-verandah door was another nail from which hung old almanacs and on top of them the latest Christmas gift from the storekeeper, a cardboard pocket for letters that was flat and in two pieces when we got it. Father had bent one of these pieces, upon which red poppies were twined round Mr. Simmons's name, and thrust its corners into slits on the larger piece, and there was the pocket. Now it was full of letters.

Two other doors opened into the kitchen. One led into my bedroom, a small box-like room with a marble-topped washstand and a single bed covered with a patchwork quilt. Through the open door I could see its newspaper-covered hessian walls that always swelled and subsided when wind buffeted the house, as if the room were breathing. Blackie, the cat, used to sleep at the foot of my bed, and Meg slept on the bag mat beside it. Sometimes, when I was asleep, mother would sneak in and hunt them out, but they always came back.

The other doorway led into Mary's and Jane's bedroom, a room the same size as mine but containing two beds and a chest-of-drawers with a swinging mirror suspended between two little top drawers in which Mary and Jane kept their brooches.

Opposite the back-verandah door was the entrance to a short passage. Worn, plush curtains closed this passageway from the kitchen, dividing the house into two sections. Here in the kitchen half you could jump on chairs and make a row and play bears under the table if you wanted to, but the front section beyond the curtains was never used for playing nor entered with dirty clothes or muddy boots.

The Front Room opened off the passage and here the linoleum shone from scrubbing and the freshly-raddled fireplace was neatly packed with wood ready for lighting on winter nights when we had visitors.

The walls of the Front Room were covered with framed photographs. There were frames made of shells, of velvet-covered wood, of pressed metal, and there was one made of cork. There were long frames containing a row of photographs and large, carved frames in one of which a fierce man with a beard stood with one hand resting on a small table standing in front of a waterfall. This was Grandfather Marshall. In the other big frame an old lady in a black lace shawl sat stiffly on a rustic seat in an arbour of roses, while behind her a thin man in narrow trousers gazed sternly at the photographer as he rested his hand on her shoulder.

These two unsmiling people were mother's parents. Father, after looking at the picture, always said grandfather had big knees like a foal, but mother said it was the narrow trousers. Whenever I now looked at the photograph, I saw grandfather's knees and thought of foals.

Father always read when sitting in the Front Room. He read *Not Guilty—A Defence of the Bottom Dog*, by Robert Blatchford, and *My Brilliant Career*, by Miles Franklin. He valued these two books that Peter Finlay had given him and often talked about them.

"I like books that tell the truth," he sometimes said. "I'd sooner be sad with the truth than happy with a lie, blowed if I wouldn't."

He came in from the loosebox, where he had been feeding the horses, and sat down on the horsehair chair that always pricked me through my trousers when I slid on it, and he said, "That last bag of chaff I got from Simmons is full of oats. It's the best bag I've had from him this year. Old Paddy O'Loughlan grew it, he reckons." He smiled at me. "How do you like being home, old chap?"

"Oo, it's good!" I told him.

"Yes, it's good all right," he said, grimacing as he tugged at his elastic-side boots. "I'll wheel you round the yard after and show you Meg's pups," he added.

"Why don't you buy some more of that chaff before it all goes?" mother suggested.

"Yes, I think I will. I'll book it up. Paddy's crop was short and all head."

"When can I have another go on my crutches?" I asked him.

"The doctor said you must lie down for an hour every day, Alan," mother reminded me.

"That's going to be a job," father muttered as he examined the soles of his boots.

"We'll have to make him."

"Yes, that's right. Don't forget now, Alan; you must lie down every day. You can have a go on your crutches every day though. I think I'll have to pad the tops with horsehair. Do they make you sore under the arms?"

"They hurt," I said.

With his boot held in front of him he looked at me for a moment with concern in his eyes.

"Pull your chair over to the table," mother said to him. She came and pushed my wheelchair to a place beside him, then stood erect and smiled down at me, "Well," she said, "we have two men back in the house again, eh! I won't have to work nearly as hard now."

11

After lunch father wheeled me round the yard. He pushed the pram close to Pat's cage and for a moment the need to clean the floor rested disturbingly on me, then I looked at Pat. The old corella was sitting hunched on his perch rubbing his bills together with the familiar grinding sound. I put my finger through the netting and scratched the back of his lowered head and the white powder from his feathers came on to my finger again and I could smell the parrot smell that always evoked the crimson flash of wings in the bush. He took my finger gently in his powerful bill and I felt the quick little tapping pushes of his dry, rubbery tongue.

"Hallo Pat," he said and his voice was mine.

And the king parrot in a cage near him still bobbed up and down, up and down on his perch, but Tom, the possum, was asleep. Father lifted him out of the dark, little box in which he slept and he opened his large, tranquil eyes and looked at me before curling up again in father's hand.

We moved over to the stable where I could hear horses

snorting chaff from their nostrils and the sharp sound of their iron shoes striking the rough stone floor as they moved.

The stable was sixty years old and seemed as if it would collapse with the weight of its straw thatch. It leaned to one side even though the uprights that supported it were trunks of sturdy gums topped by a fork in which the undressed beams of the roof were resting. It was walled with upright slabs split from the trunks of trees felled beside it and you could peer between them into the dark stalls that smelt sharply of horse manure and urine-damp straw.

Ropes tied to iron rings in the wall held the horses as they fed from feed troughs made from heavy logs hollowed with an adze and squared with a broad axe.

Beside the stable, under the same heavy, thatched roof, now noisy with nesting sparrows, was the chaff house, its rough board floor inches deep with spilt chaff. Next to it was the harness room where, on wooden brackets projecting from the slab wall, hung sets of harness—horse collars, hames, reins, breechings and saddles. Father's buckjump saddle, a Kinnear, hung on a special peg, its projecting knee pads waxed and shining.

At the foot of the wall, resting on the grooved and squared log supporting the slab uprights were tins of neatsfoot oil, harness black, bottles of turpentine, Solomon's Solution and drenches. Currycombs and brushes lay on a shelf built on to the wall and two curled stockwhips hung on nails beside it.

The thatched roof continued over the buggy shed where a three-seated buggy and the brake were kept. The brake was tipped back and the two long, hickory shafts passed under the eaves and pointed towards the sky.

The back door of the stable led into the horse yard, a circular enclosure fenced with rough-hewn seven-foot posts and split rails. This high fence sloped outwards so that a bucking horse could not scrape father's legs against the rails or crush him against the post. In front of this yard grew an old, red gum tree. In blossoming time flocks of lorikeets searched its flowers for honey, sometimes hanging upside down on the outer branches or circling the tree in screeching groups when startled into flight. Against its twisted trunk leant the broken wheel of a dray, rusty waggon axles, buggy springs with broken shackles and the weather-worn seat of a gig from the torn cushions of which projected tufts of grey horsehair. A pile of worn and rusted horseshoes rested against one of its uncovered roots.

A clump of wattles grew in one corner of the yard and beneath them horse manure lay thick on the ground, for the horses father was breaking camped here in the shade when the days were hot. Each stood with a lowered head and a lax hind leg and they switched their tails at the flies brought there by the smell of the manure.

Close to the wattles was the road gate and across the dirt roadway was an area of bushland, a refuge for the few kangaroos that still refused to retreat back to less settled areas. The messmate and stringybark trees sheltered patches of swamp where black ducks gathered and from where the booming of bitterns could be heard on still nights.

"The bunyip is out tonight," father would say when he heard them, but they made me afraid.

The store, post office and school were almost a mile away along the road and here the cleared land was squared with rich dairy farms owned by Mrs. Carruthers.

A large hill, Mt. Turalla, rose behind the township. It was covered in bracken and scrub and at the top was a crater down which the children rolled boulders that went bounding and crashing through ferns till they came to rest on the bottom far below.

Father had ridden to the top of Mt. Turalla many times. He said that horses reared on its slopes were always sure-footed and worth a couple of quid more than those reared on the flats.

After he told me this it became one of my convictions, solid within me like a rock. Everything father told me about horses was retained firmly in my mind and became part of it like my name.

"I have a half-draught colt here," he said as he pushed my pram into the stable. "It shows the whites of its eyes and I've never known a horse that showed the whites of its eyes that wouldn't kick the eye out of a mosquito if it got half a chance. It belongs to Brady. It'll kill him one day, you mark my words."

"Whoa there!" he called to the horse that had flinched forward with a flattened rump. "See! He's ready to lash out now. I've mouthed him, he's not going to be hard in the mouth, but I'll bet he'll go to market when I get him in the brake."

He left me and, moving over to the horse, ran his hand down its quivering rump.

"Steady, now. Whoa there. Whoa, old boy. Steady . . ." He talked gently to the horse and in a moment it stood quietly and turned its head to look at him.

"I'll put a kicking strap on him when I harness him up," he said. "That look means nothing."

"Can I go with you when you put him in, dad?" I asked him.

"Well, yes, you could," he said slowly as he began to fill his pipe. "You could help me break him in by holding him an' that. You would be a great help to me, but," he tamped the tobacco down with his finger, "I reckon I better take him for one or two runs first. Not far . . . An' they won't be proper breaking-in runs, of course. But I'd like you to watch him from the ground first and tell me what you think of his gait when I bring him past you. I want you to do a lot of that for me— telling me how they go an' that. You've got a feel for a horse. I don't know anybody that's got as good a feel for a horse as you have."

"I'll tell you what he's like!" I exclaimed suddenly eager to help him. "I'll watch his legs like anything. I'll tell you what he does and everything. I'd like doing that, dad."

"I knew you would," he said lighting his pipe. "I was lucky to get you."

"How did you get me, dad," I asked him wanting to be friendly and companionable with him.

"Mother carried you round inside her for a while then you were born," he told me. "You grew like a flower beneath her heart, she says."

"Like the kittens Blackie had?" I asked.

"Yes, like that."

"It makes me feel sick, a bit."

"Yes." He paused, looking out through the stable door towards the bush, then said, "It did me, too, when I first heard of it, but after a while it seems good like. You can't beat seeing a foal running beside its mother, pressing against her—you know . . . They push against her while they run." He pushed against the post to show me. "Well, she carried it before it was born. And it bucks round her like it wanted to get back. It's a good thing, I reckon. It's better than just being brought to your mother. It's well thought out when you come to think of it."

"Yes, I reckon it is, too." I quickly changed my view. "I like foals."

I felt that I loved horses carrying foals.

"I wouldn't like to be just brought," I said.

"No," father answered. "Neither would I."

12

FATHER wheeled me into the yard and told me to watch him greasing the buggy.

"Did you know it was the picnic on Saturday?" he asked me as he jacked up one of the wheels.

"The picnic!" I exclaimed, excited at the thought of this annual Sunday School gathering. "Are we going?"

"Yes."

A sudden stab of disappointment changed my expression. "I won't be able to run," I said.

"No," said father, abruptly. He spun the raised wheel with a violent jerk of his hand then watched it revolving for a moment. "It doesn't matter."

I knew it did matter. He had always told me I was to be a runner and win races like he used to do. Now I couldn't be able to win any till I got better and that wouldn't be till after the picnic.

But I didn't want to make him sad so I said, "Anyway, I suppose I would have looked back again."

I had always been the smallest and youngest competitor in the children's races at the Sunday School picnic and the handicappers all co-operated to ensure I passed the tape ahead of the older and bigger boys running against me. They always gave me half-way start, an advantage I really didn't require as I could run swiftly when it was not demanded of me, but since I was never known to win a race they were always anxious to help me.

Father always entered me in these races with great confidence. On the morning of the last picnic, when I could run like other boys, he had explained exactly what I had to do when the pistol went off and I had so impressed him by my enthusiastic reaction to his advice that he had announced at the breakfast table, "Alan will win the boys' race today."

I heard this prophetic statement as one would a pronouncement of fact from a god. Dad had said I was going to win a race today so I was going to win a race today. Any other alternative was impossible. I spent the next hour before we left in announcing this fact to any horsemen who passed our gate.

The picnic ground was on the banks of Turalla Creek, three miles away, and, on this particular day a year ago, father drove us there in the three-seated buggy. I sat with mother and father in the front seat and Mary and Jane sat facing each other in the back.

The farmers and bush people driving to the picnic always regarded the journey there as providing them with an opportunity to display the quality of their horses and along the three miles to the creek buggy wheels spun and gravel flew from swinging hooves as one challenged the other to race for the glory of his horse.

The actual roadway was a metal one but following the wide stretch of grass along the three-chain road was a track made by those drivers who studied their horses. It consisted of three deep, continuous depressions in the soft earth, the two outside ones for the wheels of the vehicles and the wider, centre one for the feet of the horses. It wound round stumps, skirted ponds and squeezed between trees until at last, where some deep drain barred the way, it joined the metal again.

But never for long. It would move out again on to the grass when the obstruction was passed and continue its twisting course till it disappeared over an horizon hill.

Father always drove on this track with its dips and hollows and the buggy swayed and rocked delightfully as he "touched up" Prince with the whip.

Prince was a raking chestnut with a Roman nose but father said he could go like a bat out of hell. He was a square-gaited trotter with broad hooves and he often "struck" when trotting—the shoes of his hind feet would strike those of his front with a sharp clicking sound.

I liked to hear it. I liked my boots to squeak when I walked, for a similar reason. Squeaking boots established me as a man and Prince's clicking shoes established him as a horse that could go. Father didn't like this habit of Prince's and he had his front shoes weighted to cure him.

When Prince got on to the dirt track and felt father rein him back—"pull him together", father called it—his ears came back, his rump lowered and he threw his powerful legs in long swinging strides that made the buggy wheels sing behind him.

And I wanted to sing too for I loved the bite of the wind on my face and the sting of the thrown dirt and gravel on my cheeks. I liked to see the grip of father's hands on the reins as he strove to pass gigs and buggies in which men he knew leant forward shaking loosened reins or using their whips as they called urgently to horses straining to reach their top.

"Hup! Hup!" called father, this breaking-in cry of his carrying with it some urgent, powerful appeal that horses responded to and fled from with increasing speed.

Now, sitting in the sunshine, a rug over my knees, watching him grease the buggy, I thought of this day, a year ago, when he had beaten McPherson in a race down the Two-Mile Flat.

For some reason father never looked back at drivers who challenged him. He looked ahead down the track he was traveling, a smile on his face.

"A bad bump can throw you back a yard," he told me once.

I always looked back. It was exciting to see the head of a powerful horse at your buggy's wheel, the flare of his nostrils, the blown foam that streaked his neck.

I remembered looking back at McPherson.

"McPherson's gaining, dad," I warned him as a yellow-wheeled jinker in which a sandy-bearded man was bringing his whip down on the flanks of a pacing grey, came pounding along the metal a length to the rear of us where we sped along the dirt track now beginning to converge on the made road.

"To hell with him!" muttered father. He stood up in front of the seat, leant forward and shortened his reins then gave a quick glance ahead to where, a hundred yards away, the dirt track met the metal road in the crossing of a drain. Beyond the culvert the dirt track moved away from the road again but on the culvert only one could pass.

"Into it, you beauty!" yelled father and he flicked Prince with the whip. The big horse flattened into a more extended stride as the track drew parallel with the road.

"Get to hell out of it!" yelled McPherson. "Draw out or be damned to you, Marshall." Mr. McPherson was an elder of the Church and knew all about hell and the damned, but he didn't know very much about Prince.

"I've got you bloody well licked!" shouted father. "Hup! Hup!" And Prince gave that little bit more that father knew he had. The flying buggy cut in under the nose of McPherson's grey, skidded on to the metal, crossed the culvert in a whirl of dust and was back in the silence of the dirt track while McPherson cursed behind us, his whip still flailing.

"Blast him!" exclaimed father. "He thinks he should have beaten me. If I'd been in the brake I'd have left him standing."

Father always swore a lot on his way to the Sunday School picnic.

"Remember where we're going," mother reminded him.

"All right," said father agreeably. "Hell!" he exclaimed. "Here comes Rogers with his new roan. Hup! Hup!"

But we had topped the final rise and the picnic ground was below us. And beside it was the creek. The angled shadow of a huge railway bridge that spanned it trembled on the water and lay motionless on the wide stretch of grass that moved back from the water's edge.

Children were already playing on this flat area. Adults were bending over baskets, unpacking cups and plates, lifting cakes from nests of paper and arranging sandwiches on trays.

Horses tied to a fence that curved over a nearby rise rested with drooping heads and hanging, unbuckled harness. Some tossed nosebags as they snorted the dust from their nostrils. Below, in the shadow of the bridge, buggies and gigs with empty shafts stood in the gaps between the piles.

Father drove our buggy between two groups of these towering columns and we tumbled out almost before his "Whoa there!" and a pull on the reins had stopped the horse.

I made for the creek at a run. Just to look at it gave me pleasure. The moving water made curved ridges against the upright stems of rushes. The flat leaves of reeds moved their pointed tips to and fro on the surface and from the bottom of deep pools silver bubbles sometimes came wriggling upwards and broke on the surface amid expanding ripples.

Old redgums grew on the banks and their limbs curved

over the water, some of them so low that the current tugged at their leaves, dragging them with it then releasing them again. The dry trunks of fallen trees lay with their rooted butts on the edge of the grassed hollows where once they had stood erect. You could use these weathered root spikes as steps and climb to the top; then you could look along the trunk and see where it disappeared beneath the water. They were cracked and bleached by sun and rain and I liked to touch them, to look intently at the texture and grain of the weathered wood seeking for possum scratches or just so that I could imagine what the tree was like when it was growing.

On the far bank of the creek bullocks stood with lifted heads among the tussocks and looked at me. A blue crane rose heavily from a clump of reeds; then Mary came and told me I had to go back to the buggy and get ready for the race. This was the race I was going to win and I told her about it as I clung to her hand while we walked across the grass to where mother was sitting on the ground beside the buggy preparing lunch. She had spread a cloth on the grass and father was kneeling beside it carving slices of meat from a cold leg of lamb. He always suspected meat bought from butchers and claimed that mutton was never any good unless it came from a sheep slaughtered while it had a full stomach and was fresh from the grass.

"They get knocked about by dogs and are jammed in yards," he used to say. "They bruise the hell out of them. You can't leave a sheep go without a feed for a couple of days without it losing condition."

Now he muttered over the leg of lamb as he turned it this way and that on the plate.

"When this lamb was alive," he said to me, "it was as long in the tooth as I am. Sit down and have a bit."

After lunch I followed him round till the bell rang for the boys' race.

"Come on now and I'll lead you in," he said, suddenly turning from the man to whom he was talking. "See you later, Tom." He waved to the man and, taking my hand, he walked with me to where Peter Finlay was busily shepherding a group of boys into an orderly line.

"Back you go," Peter kept repeating, his outstretched arms moving up and down with a jerky movement as he walked up and down in front of them. "Don't jostle. Spread out. That's better. There's no hurry. Take your time. We'll let you know when to get set. Back further . . ."

"Five to four the field," father said to him as he pushed me forward.

Peter turned round. "Ah!" he exclaimed, looking down at me with an amused smile. "Is he going to jib today?" he asked father.

"No, he's rearing to go," father told him.

Peter glanced along the track upon which we were to run then said, "Shove him up near that far tussock, Bill. He'll have a chance from there." He patted me on the head. "Now you show your old man how you can go."

I was interested in all the preparation and bustle for a race I was to win. Boys jumped up and down on their mark or leant forward with their fingers on the ground. Father told me I wouldn't have to do that. I followed him down between two long lines of people. All the people I knew were standing there watching us and smiling. Mrs. Carter was there: she had given me a lolly once. Now she waved to me.

"Run hard, Alan," she called out.

"Here's the place," said father. He stopped and, bending down, took off my shoes. The grass felt you'd like to jump up and down on it when you stood on it with your shoes off. I jumped around on it.

"Steady now," father said. "A prancing horse never wins anything. Stand still here and face that tape down there." He pointed to where at the far end of the two rows of people two men were holding a tape across the track. It seemed a long way away, but I wanted to reassure him. "I'll get there as quick as anything."

"Now, listen to me, Alan." Father squatted on his heels so that his face was close to mine. "Don't forget all I've told you. When the pistol goes bang you run straight for that tape. And don't look back. As soon as you hear the bang, you run. Run hard like you do at home. I'm going to stand over there near these people. Now I'm going. Keep looking at the tape and don't look back."

"I'll get a prize when I win, won't I?" I asked him.

"Yes," he said, "now get ready. The pistol will go off in a minute."

He walked backwards away from me. I didn't like him going away. There were too many things to remember when he wasn't there.

"Ready!" he suddenly called out to me from where he stood in front of a line of people.

I looked back to see why the pistol didn't go off. All the boys were standing in a line. I was out of all the fun up there on my own and I wished I was back with them. Then the pistol went off and they were all running. It shocked me to see how quickly they began to run. They were racing with their heads back but they hadn't started to race me yet. You can't race anybody when they're not with you.

Father was yelling "Run! Run! Run!"

Now they were all round me and it was time to race them but they wouldn't wait for me and I ran desperately after them feeling angry and a little bewildered. The tape was down when I reached it and I stopped and cried. Father ran to me and lifted me in his arms.

"Dash me rags!" he exclaimed in exasperation. "Why didn't you run when the gun went off? You looked back and waited for the boys again."

"I had to wait for them to race them," I sobbed. "I don't like winning races on my own."

"Well, don't cry over it," he said, "we'll make a runner of you yet."

But that was a year ago.

Maybe he thought of this as he spun the wheel of the buggy and I sat there in my pram watching him with a rug over my crippled legs.

"You won't be able to run this time," he said at last, "but I want you to watch them running. You stand near the tape. Run with them while you watch them. When the first kid breasts the tape you breast it with him."

"How, dad?" I did not quite understand what he meant.

"Think it," he said.

I thought over what he said while he went into the harness room for a tin of axle grease. When he came out he placed it on the ground beside the buggy then wiped his hands on a piece of rag and said, "I had a black bitch once—a half-bred kangaroo dog. She could run like the son of a gun. She could

90

stay with any flying doe and'd bail up an old man 'roo in a hundred yards. She'd scatter a mob then race up on one and toss it by grabbing the butt of its tail while it was in the air. She never went for their shoulder like other dogs. But she never missed. She was the best dog I've ever had. A bloke offered me a fiver for her once."

"Why didn't you sell her, dad?" I asked.

"Well, you see, I reared her from when she was a pup. I called her Bessie."

"I wish we had her now, dad," I said.

"Yes, I do, too, but she got staked in the shoulder and put it out or something. She had a hell of a lump on it afterwards. She was never any good after that. But I took her out just the same and she did all the barking and the other dogs did all the running. I've never seen a dog get so excited over a course. And she never chased them herself, mind you.

"I remember how we bailed up an old man 'roo once and he had his back to a tree and when Brindle—he was another kangaroo dog I had—when Brindle went in the 'roo ripped him from his shoulder to his flank and Bessie yelped as soon as the 'roo got him. By hell, she did! I've never seen a dog throw herself into scraps and courses like her. Yet she only did it by barking an' that."

"I like you telling me about her, dad," I said, eager to hear more.

"Well, you've got to be like her. Fight and run and race and ride and yell your bloody head off while you're looking on. Forget your legs. I'm going to forget them from now on."

13

THE children who lived further down our road called for me each morning and pushed me to school in the pram. They liked doing it because each one had turns in riding with me.

Those pulling the pram would prance like horses and I would yell out, "Hup! Hup!" and wave an imaginary whip.

There was Joe Carmichael, who lived almost opposite us—he was my mate—and Freddie Hawk, who could do everything better than anyone else and was the hero of the school, and "Skeeter" Bronson, who always said that he'd "tell on you" when you hit him.

Two girls lived up our road; Alice Barker was one. All the boys at the school wished she was their girl but she liked Freddie Hawk. Maggie Mulligan was the other girl. She was a big girl and knew three terrible swears and would say the three of them together if you got her wild. She would clip you on the ear as quick as look at you and I liked her wheeling me in the pram better than anyone else because I loved her.

Sometimes, when we played "bucking horses" the pram tipped over and Maggie Mulligan would say the three swears and pick me up and call to the others, "Here! Help me chuck him back before someone comes."

She had two long red plaits down her back, and sometimes boys at school would yell out, "Ginger for pluck" at her and she would sing back at them, "Long nose eats the fruit. You're lousy as a bandicoot."

She wasn't frightened of any boy and she wasn't frightened of bulls either.

When McDonald's bull got out and started fighting with one of the road bulls we all stopped to watch them. McDonald's bull was the biggest and he kept pushing the road bull backwards till he got him against a tree then he drove at his flanks. The road bull bellowed and turned to get away. Blood was running down his back legs and he made up the road towards us with McDonald's bull on his heels, goring him as he ran.

Joe and Freddie and Skeeter lit out for the fence but Maggie Mulligan stopped with me and wouldn't let go the pram handle. She tried to pull me off the track but she didn't have time and McDonald's bull gave a side toss with its horns as it passed and sent the pram flying, but I fell on ferns and wasn't hurt and Maggie Mulligan wasn't hurt either.

But the wheel of the pram was buckled and Maggie Mulligan put the Fireman's Lift on me and carried me home and she only had four spells because Joe and Freddie counted them.

At school they always left my pram near the door and I walked into the schoolroom on my crutches.

The school was a long, stone building with high, narrow windows and you couldn't see out of them when you were sitting down. They had wide sills covered with chalk dust. In one of these alcoves stood an old vase with some dead flowers in it.

There were two long blackboards, one at each end of the room.

Beneath each blackboard were ledges on which rested pieces of chalk, dusters to clean the board, large setsquares and rulers.

A fireplace full of dirty record books was let into the wall between the two blackboards, and above the fireplace was a picture of a group of blood-stained soldiers in red coats, all looking outwards and leaning forward with their rifles projecting over the dead bodies of other soldiers lying limply at their feet. In the centre of the group, higher than the others, stood a man holding a banner on a long pole. He was yelling out something and shaking his fist. It was called "The Last Stand" but Miss Pringle didn't know where they were standing. Mr. Tucker said it represented British heroism in full flower and he tapped the picture with a long stick when he said it so that you would know what he was talking about.

Miss Pringle taught the Little Ones and Mr. Tucker taught the Big Ones. Miss Pringle had grey hair and looked at you over her glasses. She wore a high whale-bone collar that made it hard for her to nod her permission for you to go out and I was always wanting to go out because then you could stand in the sun and look at Mt. Turalla and hear magpies. Sometimes there were three of us outside together and we would row over who was to go back first.

Mr. Tucker was the head teacher. He did not wear glasses. His eyes frightened you even when you hung your head and refused to face them. They were sharp and hard and cold and he used them like a whip. He always washed his hands in an enamel basin in the corner of the room and after he had washed them he would walk over to his desk and stand behind it looking at the pupils while he dried them on a small, white towel. He dried each finger separately, beginning with the first finger. His fingers were long and white and threaded on sinews you could see beneath the skin. He rubbed them briskly without losing the effect of deliberation and as he rubbed them he looked at us with his eyes.

No one moved while he dried his hands, no one spoke. When he finished he would fold the towel and put it in the desk drawer and then he would smile at us with his teeth and lips.

He terrified me as a tiger would.

He had a cane and before he used it on a boy he would swish it twice through the air and then draw it through his closed hand as if to clean it.

"Now," he would say, and his teeth would be smiling.

To be able to stand the cuts was evidence of superiority. Boys who cried from the cuts were thereafter unable to boss any other boy in the playground. Even smaller boys stood up to them, confident they could lick them. My pride demanded I establish myself in some field children valued and since most of these fields were closed to me I developed a disdainful attitude towards being caned even though I had a greater fear of Mr. Tucker than most of the pupils. I refused to jerk my outstretched hand back as the cane came down, as some boys did, nor did I grimace and fold my arms after each cut, having no faith that it eased the pain or made Mr. Tucker give you fewer cuts than he intended. After the cane I could not clasp the hand-grips of my crutches, my numbed fingers refusing to bend, so I placed the backs of my hands beneath the grips and could get back to my seat in that way.

Miss Pringle did not use a cane. She used a broad strap, split at the end into three narrow tails. These tails were supposed to sting more than a single strap but she soon discovered that this was not so and thereafter she held the strap by its divided end and belted us with the broad section.

She kept her lips tightly closed and didn't breathe when she wielded the strap but she couldn't hit very hard. She often carried it round the class with her, striking her skirt with it now and then in the way a stockman cracked a whip to frighten cattle.

She was calm when she strapped you but Mr. Tucker was seized with a savage urgency when he felt called upon to flog a boy. He would bound to his desk and fling back the broad lid with a bang, yelling, as he searched for the cane among the roll books and papers in the desk, "Come out here, Thompson. I saw you pull a face when you thought my back was turned."

No one worked when he caned a boy. We all watched in a stricken silence, numbed by fear of an anger we could not understand or explain. His reddened face and changed voice seemed to us evidence of terrible intentions and we quaked in our seats.

We knew how he saw Thompson pull a face behind his back. The glass on the picture above the fireplace reflected those behind him and when he looked at it he did not see the dead soldiers or the man screaming as he clutched the flag; he saw the faces of the children.

The children often discussed the cane and the strap. One or two of the older boys spoke with authority on the subject and we listened to them with respect.

They would remind us that a horse hair placed in a tiny split at the end of the cane would split the entire cane in two after the first blow on a boy's hand. Hearing this, I would have dreams of climbing through the window of the deserted school, inserting the horse hair and escaping unnoticed. I could see, next day, the thwarted, furious expression on Mr. Tucker's face as he gazed at the split and useless cane in his hand while I stood smiling, with outstretched hand in front of him waiting for the blow I knew he could not deliver. It was a most satisfying picture.

But to insert that horse hair meant breaking open the locked desk and this we could not do. So we rubbed resin on the palms of our hands, believing that this rendered the hand so tough no cut could hurt it.

I gradually became the authority on resin, describing the amount to use, the method of application, the varying qualities of resin, in a tone that showed I was a veteran and could not be contradicted.

But, later, I turned to wattlebark, soaking my hands in the brown liquid made from pouring hot water over the bark. I claimed this tanned the hands, and displayed my palms, calloused from constant rubbing on the crutch grips, to prove it. I made many converts and a bottle of wattlebark liquid was worth four marbles or six cigarette cards provided it was almost black.

At first I sat in the gallery at Miss Pringle's end of the room. The gallery consisted of rows of desks standing on rising tiers till, at the rear, they had risen half-way to the roof. The desks each held six children and had backless seats attached to them. They were disfigured by initials, circles, squares and gashes carved into the wood with pocket knives. Some had round holes cut through the top and you could drop a rubber or pencil through into the open compartment below. Six inkwells rested in holes bored to secure them and there were grooves beside these inkwells for holding pens and pencils.

The Little Ones used slates to write upon. The slates had a hole bored through the top of the frame, and a string, to which a piece of rag was tied, was passed through this hole and tied to the slate.

When you wanted to clean the slate you spat on it and rubbed the writing away with the rag. After a while the rag began to smell and you got a new piece from your mother.

It was the custom to work up a good spit by sucking the inside of your cheeks and working your jaws. A big spit was reason for pride and you showed it to the boy next to you before you tilted the slate and guided the moving spittle this way and that till the wet trail it left behind it reduced it to a size where further experiment was boring. You then wiped your slate with the rag and paid attention to Miss Pringle.

Miss Pringle believed that constant repetition of a fact

embedded it in your mind for ever, complete with full understanding of all it implied.

You first learned the alphabet by repeating it each day, then in a sing-song voice the whole class chanted, "C-A-T, cat; C-A-T, cat; C-A-T, cat."

That night you told your mother you could spell "cat" and she thought it was wonderful.

But my father didn't. He said, "To hell with 'cat'! Spell 'horse'," when I confronted him with my new knowledge.

I learned quickly when I set my mind to it but I was a giggler and a talker and was constantly being caned. I left each class with something still unlearned and I began to hate school. My writing was bad, according to Miss Pringle, and she always clucked her tongue when she looked at my spelling. Freehand Drawing appealed to me because then I could draw gum leaves and my drawings would be different from everyone else's. For Ruled Drawings we drew cubes and mine were never square.

Once a week we were given a lesson called "Science". I liked this lesson because then we were allowed to stand round the table and you could push and shove and have fun.

Mr. Tucker opened the cupboard containing some glass tubes, a spirit lamp, a bottle of mercury and a leather disc with a piece of string attached to the centre. He placed these things on the table and said, "Today we are concerned with the weight of air which is fourteen pounds to the square inch."

This didn't make sense to me but the fact that I was standing beside Maggie Mulligan made me wish to shine so I proffered the information that my father had told me the fuller you are with air the lighter you are and you couldn't sink in the river. I thought this had some bearing on the subject but Mr. Tucker slowly put the piece of leather back on the table then looked at me with his eyes so that I could not face him and said through his teeth, "Marshall, I would have you know that we are not interested in your father or in any observation made by your father even if such observations proclaim the stupidity of his son. Would you please attend to the lesson."

He then wet the leather disc and pressed it on the desk and none of us could pull it off except Maggie Mulligan who ripped the guts out of it with one yank and proved air didn't weigh anything.

She told me when she was wheeling me home that what I said was right and that air weighed nothing.

"I wish I could give you a present," I told her, "but I haven't got anything."

"Have you got any comics?" she asked.

"There's two under my bed," I said eagerly. "I'll give you both of them."

14

M Y crutches were gradually becoming a part of me. I had developed arms out of proportion to the rest of my body and my armpits were now tough and hard. The crutches did not chafe me any more and I could walk without discomfort.

I practised different walking styles, calling them by the names applied to the gaits of horses. I could trot, pace, canter and gallop. I fell frequently and heavily but learned to throw myself into positions that saved my bad leg from injury. I typed the falls I had and when beginning to fall always knew whether it would be a "bad" or "good" fall. If both crutches slipped when I was well advanced on my forward swing I fell backwards and this was the worst fall of all since it often resulted in my being winded or twisting my bad leg beneath me. It was a painful fall and I used to thump the earth with my hands to keep from crying out when I fell in this manner. When only one crutch slipped or struck a stone or root, I fell forward on to my hands and was never hurt.

I was never free of bruises or lumps or gravel rashes and each evening found me attending to some injury I had received that day.

But they did not distress me. I accepted these annoying inconveniences as being part of normal living and I never for a moment regarded them as a result of being crippled, a state which, at this period, I never applied to myself.

I began walking to school and became acquainted with exhaustion—the state so familiar to cripples and their constant concern.

I always cut corners, always made in as straight a line as I could to where I wanted to go. I would walk through clumps of thistles rather than go round them, climb through fences rather than deviate a few yards to go through a gate.

A normal child expends its surplus energy by cavorting, skipping, spinning in circles or kicking stones along the ground as it walks up the street. I, too, felt the need to do this and I indulged in clumsy caperings and leaps as I walked up the road just because of a need to express how well I felt. People seeing me expressing my joy in living so clumsily regarded it as pathetic and stared at me with pity so that I immediately stopped till they were out of sight then threw myself into my happy world again, free from their sadness and their pain.

Though I was not aware of it, my values were changing and from having a natural respect for those boys who spent most of their time reading, I became absorbed in physical achievement. I admired a football player, a boxer, a bikerider far more than those with impressive mental achievements. The tough boys became my playmates and my conversation often suggested aggressiveness.

"I'll punch you fair in the eye after school, Ted; you see if I don't."

I talked in terms of violence yet shrank from demonstrating it. I could not punch a boy in the eye unless he first punched me.

Violence of any kind was abhorrent to me. Sometimes, after seeing a man flog a horse or kick a dog, I would creep home and put my arm around Meg's neck and hold her tightly for a moment. It made me feel better as if her security embraced myself.

Animals and birds were never long out of my mind. Birds in flight affected me like music. I watched dogs running, with an almost painful awareness of the beauty of their motion, and a galloping horse made me tremble with some emotion I could not define.

I was not aware that in this worship of all action that suggested power and strength I was building up a compensation for an inability to indulge in such action myself. I only knew I felt an uplift of spirit when I witnessed it.

Joe Carmichael and I hunted rabbits and hares together and with a pack of dogs we went tramping through the bush and across open paddocks, and when we roused the hare and the dogs gave chase I watched with a keen pleasure the kangaroo dog's undulating run, his lowered head close to the ground, the magnificent curve of his neck and shoulders and the swinging, leaning turn of him as he came round after the dodging hare.

I began walking into the bush in the evenings so that I could smell the earth and the trees. I knelt among the moss and fern and pressed my face against the earth, breathing it into me. I dug among the roots of grass with my fingers, feeling an intense interest in the texture of the earth I was holding, the feel of it, the fine, hair-like roots it contained. It seemed magical to me and I began to feel that my head was too far above it to appreciate to the fullest the grass and wildflowers and ferns and stones along the tracks I walked. I wanted to be like a dog, running with my nose to the earth so that there would be no fragrance missed, no miracle of stone or plant unobserved.

I would crawl through ferns by the swamp's edge, making tunnels of discovery through the undergrowth, or lie prone with my face close to the curled fronds of bracken newly emerged from the creative darkness of the earth, gently clasped like babies' hands. Oh! the tenderness of them; the kindness and compassion of them. I would lower my head and touch them with my cheek.

But I felt confined, restricted in my quest for some revelation that would explain and appease the hunger I possessed. So I created dreams, for in these I could roam as I willed, unhampered by an unresponsive body.

After tea, before it was time to go to bed, in that first expectant darkness when the frogs from the swamp began their chirping and early possums peered out from hollow limbs, I would stand at our gate looking through the rails at the bush across the road where it stood motionless against the sky, waiting for the night. Beyond it Mt. Turalla hid the rising moon on those nights I loved the best and its huge shoulder was sharp against the glow.

Listening to the frogs or a mopoke or the chirr of a possum, I would launch myself out into a powerful run through the night, galloping on four legs, my nose to the earth as I followed a rabbit's trail or the tracks of a kangaroo. Maybe I was a dingo or just a dog living a life of its own in the bush—I was never quite sure—but I was never separate from the bush through which I loped in tireless strides. I was part of it and all that it offered was mine.

In this escape from the reality of laborious walking I experienced speed that was tireless, leaps and bounds that were effortless and the grace of movement I recognised in men in action and in the running of dogs and horses.

As a dog running through the night I experienced no effort, no fatigue, no painful falls. I raced through the bush with my nose to the leaf-strewn earth, bounded a length behind speeding kangaroos, turning as they did, leaping to bring them down, hurtling over logs and creeks, passing from moonlight to shadow, twisting and turning, my body firm with tireless muscle and animated by an intense and joyful energy.

In my hunting dreams my imagination stopped at the seizing of a rabbit or kangaroo; it was the chase in which I gloried, the merging of my identity with the bush.

I could not imagine exhaustion in uncrippled bodies. Exhaustion, to me, was a condition arising from walking on crutches and had no part in the lives of normal people. It was my crutches that prevented me running all the way to school without stopping, that increased the beat of my heart when I climbed a hill, and made me cling panting to a tree while other boys continued on. But I didn't resent my crutches. I could not feel that way. I left them behind in my dreams but I returned to them without resentment.

In this period of adjustment the two worlds in which I lived were equally as enjoyable. I gained from each the stimulus to pass into the other. The world of reality forged me; in the world of dreams I swung the blade.

15

FREDDIE HAWK could run and fight and climb and use a shanghai better than anyone else in the school. He was a champion at marbles and could pitch a cigarette card further than the other boys. He was a quiet boy who never boasted and I was devoted to him. He was saving cigarette cards and only had one to get to complete the set of "Arms and Armour of the British Empire".

He kept this set in a tobacco tin and once or twice a day he would take out the little pack, wet his thumb, and count them while I watched him. There were always forty-nine.

I wanted to get him that missing card and would accost every man I met: "Got any cigarette cards, mister?" but without result.

After I had concluded that it must be the rarest cigarette card in the world, a horseman I stopped as he was passing our gate drew it from a packet and gave it to me.

I could hardly believe I had it. I read the number several times—thirty-seven; that was right. Freddie didn't have number thirty-seven.

Next day I waited impatiently on the road for him to appear and began yelling the news to him when he was a quarter of a mile away. When he was close enough to hear me he began to run and when he came up I handed him the card.

"I got it from a bloke on a horse," I told him excitedly. "He says to me, 'What are you saving?' and I says to him, 'Arms and Armour of the British Empire,' and he says, 'By hell I might have one of them!' and by hell, he did too. Now you've got the set."

Freddie looked at the card then turned it over and looked at the number. He then read through the description of the Armour it pictured and remarked, "It's it all right, b' cripes!"

He took his tobacco tin from his pocket and opened it. He placed the new card in its correct position in the pack, tapped the pack on a post to straighten it, licked his thumb, and counted the cards slowly, saying each number aloud. I repeated the number with him.

"Fifty!" I exclaimed triumphantly at the end of the count.

"It looks like it," he said.

He again tapped the pack against the post and counted them again, beginning with the last one.

"Now you've got the set, Freddie," I said happily when he had finished. "And they're all goodies."

"Yes," he said. He placed the pack back into the tobacco tin. "Fancy—the bloody set." He held the tin at arm's length and looked at it, smiling.

"Here, take it," he said, suddenly thrusting the tin into my hands. "They're yours. I saved 'em for you."

He rarely played with me at school, being too intent winning marbles or cigarette cards or spinning tops.

I was a poor marbles player and always lost. Freddie had a Milky Really worth a bob and he gave it to me so that I could play "Reallies Up". Each boy competing placed a Really in the ring but only the best players would risk such valuable marbles. Each time I played I lost the Milky Really and I would go to Freddie and say, "I lost it again, Freddie."

"Who to?" he would ask.

"Billy Robertson."

"All right," Freddie would say and he would go and win it back for me and say, "Here it is," then he would return to his own game again.

He always moved over when I was having a row with a boy and he would stand there listening while he kicked the gravel with his foot. Once when Steve McIntyre told me he'd kick me on the backside, I said to him, "It's the last backside you'll ever kick," and Steve got back to take a run at me. Freddie had been listening and he said to Steve, "The bloke that boots him boots me."

Steve didn't want to kick me after that but when we were marching into school he whispered to me, "I'll get you after school, see if I don't." I lashed out with my crutch and got him on the shin before he drew back and after that all the kids began taking sides and some said I wanted a punch on the nose and some said Steve wanted one.

My row with Steve had started when we were all struggling to get a drink at the square iron tank that held the school's water supply. A large tin pannikin with a rusted bottom hung on the tap and beneath the tap the spilt water had collected in a depression worn by the boots of the children. Those clamouring for a drink stamped in this muddy pool like cattle at a trough.

At playtime in the summer there was a rush for the tank, girls and boys pushing and shoving, grabbing the half-full pannikin from the lips of those already drinking and pouring the contents down their own throats while a score of hands were reaching towards them. As the drinking ones discarded the pannikin it was seized and drained by others.

There was a constant yelling for recognition. The one drinking was appealed to, threatened, denounced or reminded of obligations he had forgotten.

"Here on the outside, Bill . . . I'm here . . . Hand it over. I lent you my Really. After you, Jim . . . Hey, Jim, after you . . . There's enough in it for the two of us. Get out of the bloody road, look who you're pushing . . . I got here first. I'm next. You go to hell!"

Water was spilt down dresses, shirts . . . Boys emerged hopping on one leg and holding shins with their clasped hands: "Oo-oo-oo." Girls yelled, "I'll tell on you." Those who had drunk forced their way out from the crush wiping their wet mouths with the backs of their hands and grinning triumphantly.

I fought with the others. In matters such as this no concessions were made to my crippled limbs and I was knocked over or pushed aside with complete disregard of my crutches.

I encouraged this attitude by talking in terms inappropriate to my powers. "I'll fix you in a minute," I would threaten the school bully to his astonishment.

It was recognised that I was prepared to follow up my threats by action but until my row with Steve McIntyre I never had to make good my threats.

Steve hit the pannikin upwards when I was drinking and soaked me with water and grabbed the pannikin out of my hand. I punched him in the stomach then fell over since it jerked the crutch from beneath my arm. While on the ground I grabbed his legs and tipped him into the mud. But he got up before I did and was going to have a go at me then but the bell rang.

For a week after that we exchanged threats, each surrounded by a group of mates whispering advice. It was recognised that I had powerful arms and Steve's advisers openly proclaimed that if you kicked the crutches from beneath me I was done. This was denied by the boys on my side who were of the opinion that I was at my best when on the ground.

I didn't know when I was at my best but I was completely incapable of thinking in terms of defeat.

"Say he knocks me out," I explained to Freddie Hawk. "Well, when I come round I'll have another go at him."

My reasoning was based on a simple premise, "If you don't give in, you're never beaten." Since nothing on earth would make me give in I must win.

Freddie, counting marbles into a cloth bag with a tape on it remarked, "I'll fight him for you and I'll give you another Really."

I couldn't agree to this. I wanted Steve McIntyre for myself. I had to fight him or else I would be a siss. If I didn't fight him the kids would never again take any notice of what I said.

I explained this to Freddie who then suggested I fight him with my back against a stone wall, because then, whenever he missed me, he would bash his hands against the stones.

I thought this was a good idea.

When I got home from school that night I told mother I was going to fight Steve McIntyre behind the old stump in Jackson's paddock next day.

She turned from the stove where she was cooking and exclaimed, "Fight? Are you going to fight?"

"Yes," I said.

She shifted the big black kettle on the stove and said, "I don't like you fighting, Alan. Can't you get out of it?"

"No," I said. "I want to fight him."

"Don't," she pleaded with me, then suddenly stopped and looked at me with a troubled expression arrested on her face while she stood thinking.

"I . . . What does your father say?"

106

"I haven't told him yet."

"Go down and tell him now."

I walked down to the stockyard where father was walking round and round behind a young, nervous horse that was dragging a post behind it. The horse's neck was arched and there was froth around its mouth where it champed the mouthing bit. It moved in starts and father kept talking to it.

I climbed on to the rail and said, "I'm going to fight Steve McIntyre tomorrow."

Father reined the horse in and moved up to it where he began patting its neck.

"How do you mean—fight?" he asked. "Are you having a go at him with your fists?"

"Yes."

"What's the row over?"

"He chucked water over me."

"That's not so bad, is it?" he asked. "I like water fights, myself."

"He keeps chipping me."

"Well, that's not too good," he said slowly, looking at the ground. "Who's back-stopping you?"

"Freddie Hawk."

"Yes," he murmured to himself. "He's all right," then added, "I suppose you've got to lock horns with someone." He looked up at me. "You don't go round looking for fights, do you, son? I wouldn't like to think that."

"No," I said. "He picks me."

"I see," he said. He looked at the horse. "Wait till I let this colt go."

I watched him unfasten the breast plate and drop the trace chains; then I climbed from the fence and waited for him at the stable door.

"Now, let's get this straight," he said when he came out. "How big's this McIntyre kid? I don't remember him."

"He's bigger than me but Freddie reckons he's got a tail."

"Yes," argued father, "but what happens when he hits you? He'll play hell with you while he keeps out of reach. You might get one chop at him but a lift under the chin'd flatten you like a tack. And not because you can't fight, mind you," he hastened to add. "You're the sort of bloke who could go like a threshin' machine. But how are you going to keep standing? How do you hang on to your crutches and paste him at the same time?"

"Once I'm down I'm set," I told him eagerly. "I'll pull him down then. He'll never get away."

"How about your back?"

"It's all right. It doesn't hurt. If he kicked me on it, it'd hurt, but I'll lie on it."

Father took out his pipe and looked thoughtfully at his fingers pressing tobacco into the bowl.

"Pity you couldn't fight him some other way. How'd you go with shanghais or something like that?"

"Oo! He's good with a shanghai," I hastened to inform him. "He can kill a tomtit across the road."

"How about sticks?" father suggested doubtfully.

"Sticks!" I exclaimed.

"Well, if you had a go at him with sticks, you've got something your way. You're stronger in the arms than he is. You could sit down facing him on the grass and have a lash at him that way. When they say 'Go!' or whatever they say, king him. If he's yellow like you say he'll toss it in after he collects that first hit."

"What if he won't fight with sticks?"

"Just work him along to have a lick at you with sticks," father explained. "If he still jibs at it, call him yellow in front of the other boys. He'll rise to that hook. Take him gently. Don't lose your temper. Swipe him on the knuckles if you can. If he's like his old man he's a soda. I see his old man down at the pub the other day poking in as if he'd like to have a go at someone. When old Riley invited him out on the grass he closed up. This kid'll be like him. You see the look on him when you tell him it's sticks not fists."

That night, through the open door of my bedroom, I saw father talking to mother as she sat darning my stockings, and I heard him say to her, "We've just got to toughen him, Mary. You know that. He's got to learn to take it on the chin no matter how it's dished out. Save him from this and he's going to get it fair in the neck later on. It's a cow, but there you are. We got to cut out working for the kid; we got to work for the man. I want him to try the lot no matter what the risk. Half the time it's a matter of risking his neck or breaking his heart; I choose to risk his neck. That's how I see it anyway. I may be wrong, but I'm staking all I've got, I'm right."

Mother said something in reply and he answered, "Yes, I know, I know. We've got to take that risk. It frightens hell out of me too but I reckon the worst he'll get is a lump on the head and a cut or two." He paused, then added, "I wouldn't like to be the kid McIntyre," and he threw back his head and laughed gently with the lamp light on his face while mother watched him.

16

Fights were always held after school. On those days when a fight was to take place an air of excitement and tension seized each child and the girls kept threatening to "tell" and the school's known tell-tale-tits were subjected to a tirade of abuse that resulted in offended girls switching their pigtails and marching off with their noses in the air while those pupils who despised the tell-tale watched them balefully.

But it took courage to tell when almost the entire school were in favour of the fight and those girls with reputations as betrayers made a few bluffing marches to the school door where they stopped in indecision and exchanged slanderous remarks about the pigs of boys watching them.

The girls did not attend the fights, it being considered too brutal an exhibition for their genteel minds but they watched from a distance and swore excitedly among themselves, so Maggie Mulligan told me.

She always came to the fights. She walked with the group that surrounded me on our march to Jackson's paddock and took the opportunity to convey her allegiance to me in a hurried whisper, "If he licks you, I'll lick his sister." No remark could have established her loyalty more.

"I'll belt hell out of him," I told her confidently.

I had no doubts as to the outcome. I was an interested observer rather than the central figure of the preparations made by the boys on my side. The division in loyalties was quite plain. Each boy had been asked whose side he was on and the school was about equally divided.

Steve McIntyre had, at first, scorned to fight with sticks but the suggestion had been so enthusiastically received by all the boys who heard me make it that he couldn't very well refuse especially after I had denounced him as yellow and given him the "Coward's Blows" by tapping him three times on the shoulder while I chanted, "One-two-three you can't fight me."

So sticks it was, and Freddie Hawk cut me a beauty. The wattle from which it had been cut had no grubs in it, so Freddie told me in the manner of an authority. It was three feet long and thick at one end.

"Hold it by the thin end," Freddie ordered. "Swing it like you're going to hit a cow. Get him behind the ear, then swipe him another on the nose."

I listened with respect to Freddie. I was sure there was nothing he did not know.

"Behind the ear is a good place," I agreed.

Spies brought information from one camp to another and it was said Steve was going to hit straight down "like he was chopping wood!"

"There's only going to be two hits," he boasted. "I'll hit him and he'll hit the ground."

"Like hell!" Freddie greeted this information from a reliable informer with contempt. "What's Alan doing while he's chopping him!"

Freddie and Joe Carmichael who were back-stopping for me had measured the sticks, one against the other, so that neither of us would have an advantage.

Steve's supporters surrounded him in a compact group when we were all gathered behind the big stump in Jackson's paddock. Maggie Mulligan reckoned Steve was showing signs he'd like to quit. But Freddie didn't.

"He fights best when he's howlin'," he told me, "and he ain't howlin' yet."

Before Steve and I sat down opposite each other, Steve took off his coat, rolled up his shirt sleeves and spat on his hands. This impressed everybody except Maggie Mulligan who reckoned he was showing off.

I didn't take off my coat because my shirt had a lot of holes in it and I didn't want Maggie Mulligan to see them. But I spat on my hands just to show I knew it was the right thing to do, then I folded my legs beneath me like a Blackfellow and swung the stick through the air as if I was Mr. Tucker swishing his cane.

111

After Steve finished spitting on his hands he sat opposite me, out of reach of my stick, so they made him come closer. I reached out my stick to see if I could reach his head and I could easily, so I said I was set. Steve reckoned he was set, too, then Freddie gave his final instructions.

"Remember," he said, "nobody is to tell old Tucker about this."

Everybody promised not to tell old Tucker then Freddie said, "Into it," and Steve hit me on the head with his stick. It landed on my hair and skidded down my cheek taking skin with it and was so completely unexpected that he hit me a second time on the shoulder before I finally realised we had started.

The blows I then delivered were inspired by a terrific rage and would have stopped a bull, so Maggie Mulligan said.

Steve fell over backwards to escape them and I threw myself forward and belaboured him furiously as he tried to roll away. His nose was bleeding and he let out such a bawl of pain that I stopped in indecision but Freddie Hawk cried, "Finish him off," and I began again, crying out between each blow, "Have you had enough? Have you had enough?" until, between his howls I heard him cry, "Yes."

Joe Carmichael was standing beside me with my crutches and Freddie helped me up on to them and I was trembling like a young horse. My face was stinging and painful to touch and a lump was growing on my head.

"I beat him," I said. "Didn't I?"

"You knocked fog out of him," said Maggie Mulligan, then added, leaning anxiously towards me, "How's your bad leg?"

Father and mother were waiting at the gate when I got home. Father pretended to be mending it and he waited until the other kids went on up the road; then he came over to me quickly and asked, holding his eagerness back, "How'd you go?"

"I beat him," I said and somehow I felt like crying.

"Good on ya!" said father, then looked anxiously at my face. "He's crow-picked you bad. You look as if you've been through a threshin' machine. How're you feeling?"

"Good."

He held out his hand to me. "Shake," he said. "You've got the heart of a bullock."

When he shook my hand he said, "Now mother would like to shake it too." But mother picked me up in her arms.

Next day Mr. Tucker looked at my face then called me out and flogged me for fighting and he flogged Steve McIntyre, too, but I kept remembering that father said I had the heart of a bullock and I didn't cry out.

17

J OE CARMICHAEL lived quite close to our place. After school
hours we were rarely apart. On Saturday afternoons we
always went hunting together and on weeks nights we set
traps which we visited early each morning. We knew the names
of all the birds in the bush around our homes; we knew their
habits, their nesting places, and each of us had a collection of
eggs that we kept in cardboard boxes half full of pollard.

Joe had a fresh, ruddy face and a slow smile that made
grown-ups like him. He raised his cap to women and would
go messages for anyone. He never quarrelled but always clung
stubbornly to an opinion even though he did not defend it.

Joe's father worked for Mrs. Carruthers, doing odd jobs
round the station, and each morning in the dawn he rode past
our gate on a pony called Tony. Each evening as darkness was
falling he came riding home again. He had a sandy moustache
and father said he was the most honest man in the district.
Mrs. Carruthers paid him twenty-five shillings a week but she
took five shillings back for the rent of his house. His house
was built on an acre of land and he kept a cow.

Mrs. Carmichael was a thin, little woman with her hair
drawn back in two tight wings above her ears. It was done up
in a bun at the back. She washed clothes in round wooden
troughs made from the halves of barrels and she always
hummed a tune as she washed. The tune was always the same.
It didn't go high or low but remained on an even key like an
expression of contentment. It moved out from the washhouse
on the summer evenings and greeted me as I came through
the trees to their place and I always stood still to listen to it.

She made ketchup from the mushrooms we gathered. She

would place them evenly on a tray and sprinkle salt upon them and little pink beads of juice would gather on their gills and this was the beginning of the ketchup.

She kept fowls and ducks and geese and a pig. When the pig was big Mr. Carmichael killed it and put it in a tub of hot water and scraped the hair off it, then he salted it and hung it in a little hut made of bags. He lit fires of green leaves on the floor of this hut and smoke came out everywhere. After he did this the pig was bacon and he gave father some and father said it was the best bacon he had ever tasted.

Mrs. Carmichael always smiled at me when I came there and said, "Sure, it's you again." Then she would say, "I will give you and Joe a piece of bread and jam in a minute an' I will."

She never seemed to notice my crutches. She never mentioned them in all the years I knew her. She never looked at them or at my legs or back. She always looked at my face.

She spoke to me as if unaware that I couldn't run like other boys.

"Run down and get Joe now," she'd say, or, "You and Joe will be runnin' the fat off your bones with your rabbits and things. Sit down now and have a bite to eat."

I was always wanting her house to catch fire so that I could dash in and save her life.

Joe had a brother, Andy, who was too young to go to school. It was Joe's job to look after Andy and Joe and I regarded him as a burden.

Andy was fair and could run like a kangaroo rat. It took Joe all his time to catch him when he wanted to boot him. Andy could dodge like a hare. He was very proud of being able to dodge and sometimes threw cowdung at Joe so that Joe would chase him. Joe couldn't run much but he hung like a dog to the trail once he started. He'd wear Andy down and just as he was going to grab him, Andy would let out a wail that brought his mother dashing from the washhouse.

"What are ye up to now?" she would call. "Leave the boy alone. He's done ye no harm."

Joe propped like a stock horse when he heard his mother's voice, and Andy would scuttle off with a grin on his face and cheek Joe from behind a tree.

Joe always contrived to get Andy a long way from home when he wanted to clip his ear. But Andy's howls could be heard half a mile and Joe had to shepherd him away from the house till they died down. Joe often remarked, "Andy's not worth the worry of him," but let anyone criticise Andy and Joe would shape up and dance around like Tommy Burns.

Joe had two dogs—Dummy and Rover. Dummy was a pure-bred greyhound, a yellow dog that always yelped when you pressed his back. Joe attributed this to the fact that Dummy was once run over by a buggy and had never got over it.

"If it wasn't for him being run over," Joe often explained, "he'd win the Waterloo Cup any day."

Dummy's accident didn't affect his speed in the bush and Joe and I were given to boasting about him when discussing dogs at school.

Rover was a mongrel that displayed a toothy grin when he wagged his tail. He grovelled at your feet, turned over on his back and wriggled his devotion when you spoke to him. We thought a lot of Rover.

I never took Meg hunting but I had a kangaroo dog called Spot. Spot wasn't as fast as Dummy but he was better through scrub and had tougher feet. He had been ripped by an old man kangaroo when he was a pup and had lost his heart for kangaroos after that. But he was a good rabbiter.

With the three dogs nosing through the grass and trees ahead of us, Joe and I set off every Saturday afternoon searching for rabbits and hares. We sold the skins to a bearded skin buyer who used to drive his horse and waggon up to Joe's each week. The money we received for the skins we placed in a tin. We were saving up to buy *Leach's Bird Book* which we regarded as the most wonderful book you could possibly get.

"I suppose the Bible's better," Joe once conceded. Joe was faintly religious at times.

Beyond the belt of messmate skirting the swamp was open bush country and beyond that, the grass paddocks of farms where we were always certain of putting up a hare.

On these hunting excursions Joe adapted his pace to suit mine. When plovers rose with warning cries from clumps of tussock, he would not rush ahead to search for their nest; he

116

would walk side by side with me. He never robbed me of the pleasure of discovery. When he detected, before me, the crouched form of a hare in its seat, he would beckon me with violent gestures and make soundless contortions with his mouth that suggested urgent cries for me to hurry. I would swing towards him on my crutches, raising and lowering them with exaggerated care so that they came to rest in silence between each leap. Then we would watch it together as it crouched with its bulging, frightened eyes staring at us, its ears flattened along its back. The sound of the approaching dogs would make it tighten its ears, pressing them still lower to its hunched back till our simultaneous yell sent it in one bound on its race towards the distant rise where the long grass was.

"We'll rouse one here," I said to Joe one sunny morning when we had set off with our lunches and were threading our way through tussocky grass with Andy close behind us. "There's hundreds in here; you can tell by the look of it. Call Dummy. You keep back, Andy!"

"I want to stop with you," said Andy, a note of rebellion in his voice.

"Don't start him off before we get properly going," Joe warned me. "If he starts howling now he'll rouse every hare for miles."

Andy listened to this with satisfaction. "There won't be a hare anywhere," he agreed, nodding his head.

After a speculative glance at Andy I concluded not to press the point.

"All right," I said, "you come with me, Andy. I'm going up the rise to stop them going through the pop-hole in Baker's fence. Joe'll put 'em up. Don't let the dogs in till I yell 'right', Joe." I addressed Joe.

"Come behind here," Joe yelled at Rover. Rover crawled to Joe's feet and turned over on his back in a plea for mercy. "Get up," ordered Joe sharply.

"Come on, Andy," I ordered.

"Yes, you go with Alan, Andy," said Joe. Joe was pleased to get rid of Andy.

When I reached the wire netting fence that followed the rise, I made Andy sit down against the small round hole in the netting on the edges of which brown hairs were caught in the spikes.

"You sit there, Andy," I said, "and they won't be able to get through."

"They might charge me." Andy was a bit uncertain of the wisdom of this manoeuvre.

"Charge, be blowed!" Andy exasperated me.

I walked back a little way and yelled to Joe, "I've blocked the hole with Andy. Put one up now."

"Fetch 'em out," Joe called to the dogs.

Rover, who was always the first to discover a hare or a rabbit, suddenly threw off his humble demeanour and became full of aggressive energy. He dashed into the tussocks closely followed by Dummy and Spot who kept leaping high above the grass, their necks stretched, their heads turning as they searched the runways for that flash of fur that heralded an escaping hare.

Rover suddenly yelped and threw himself at a tussock from where a hare lifted itself in one graceful leap. The abject, cowering creature seeking to conceal itself in the grass was gone. Now its ears were erect and its run was confident. It gave three skips as if to balance itself before stretching out in a gliding run on the pad that led to the pop-hole.

Dummy, with Spot's head close to his flanks, came in silently, his body flexing like a bow. It curved and straightened with each bound; the head, independent of these movements, stretched forward with terrible purpose. For the first few yards his bounds were convulsive and made by violent effort; then he reached his running speed and moved with a curving and effortless rhythm.

Close behind him, Spot moved in similar fashion and further back the barking, yelping Rover, his long hair flopping, strove to keep them in sight, plunging through obstructing grass as if its resistance was directed and hostile.

The hare, not yet frightened into top speed by the first drive of a dog to seize it, sped along the track with its long ears fully erect, its head high. It still gave an occasional skip as it ran but near the pop-hole the yells of Andy and me scared it and it turned quickly away, dropping its ears in concealment as it sped off through the grass. Dummy, following fast, skidded round in a propping turn, the gravel flung by his tearing paws bouncing off Andy's sailor jacket and the arm with which he shielded his face.

Spot, a little to the rear, cut in behind Dummy and drove in for the kill, but the hare dodged swiftly, turning in its own length, and shot back between the two dogs. Dummy, now recovered from his turn, drew up on the hare and attempted to scoop it up in his open jaws as he over-ran it. But again the hare dodged and now, thoroughly frightened, it made off across the paddock with both dogs racing behind it.

"Sool 'im! Catch 'im!" I yelled, following in bounds across the grass.

Joe, running in on an angle, kept yelling, "Skitch 'im, boy! Skitch 'im!"

In the centre of the paddock Dummy took another turn out of the hare, then Spot, cutting a corner, brought it round once more with a drive that sent him skidding away from the hare that now made for the scrub with Dummy gaining on it with every bound.

Spot cut across towards the scrub and, as Dummy worked it round, he charged at the hare and followed it into the teatree and bracken with no slowing up of his speed.

"He'll lose him in there," Joe panted as he came up to me.

We stood and watched the line of scrub then suddenly, from deep within it, there came a loud yelp, a howl, then silence.

"He's staked," I exclaimed in fear, looking at Joe, hoping desperately that he would offer another explanation.

"Looks like it," he said.

"He'll be killed dead," said Andy in a frightened voice.

"You shut up!" snapped Joe.

We searched the scrub till we found him. He was lying on ferns with blood on his chest and the stake that pierced him had blood on it too. It was a broken-off limb of a tree, hidden by ferns and pointed like a dagger.

We covered him with scrub till you couldn't see him; then we went home and I didn't cry till I found dad in the harness room and told him.

"It's bad," he said, "I know that. But he wouldn't know what hit him."

"Would it hurt?" I asked tearfully.

"No," he answered in an assuring tone. "He wouldn't feel it. Wherever he is now he'll still think he's running." He looked at me thoughtfully for a moment then added, "He'd be a sad dog if he knew you were cut up over him sleeping on the ferns out there in the bush."

I stopped crying when he said this.

"It's only that I'll miss him," I explained.

"I know," said father gently.

18

EACH day after school Joe drove his mother's ducks and geese to a pond a quarter of a mile away and each evening he drove them back again. They moved ahead of him in a rocking, white line, alive with eagerness and anticipation. When he drove them through the last clump of trees they increased their speed and began quacking, and Joe sat down.

I nearly always accompanied him and we sat together. We both enjoyed watching the ducks with lowered breasts enter the water then glide out with the tiny waves of the pond slapping and rocking them. In the centre of the pond they stretched erect and flapped their wings then sat back in the water with a comfortable wriggle of their tails and bodies before searching for the water creatures that inhabited the pond.

Joe reckoned there could be anything in the pond but I didn't think so.

"You never know what's in there," Joe reflected at times.

On windy days we placed crews of ants in empty fish tins and sailed them across the pond, and sometimes we paddled round the edge looking for apus, that strange, shrimp-like creature with its moving gills.

Joe knew a lot about apus.

"They're very delicate," he told me. "They die if you put them in bottles."

I wondered where they went when the pond was dry.

"God only knows!" Joe said.

While the ducks were enjoying themselves we wandered in the bush looking for birds, and, in the spring, climbing to their nests.

I was fond of climbing trees. Anything in the nature of a challenge always roused me, driving me to attempt things that Joe, under no compulsion to prove his physical fitness, would not wish to do.

I used my arms in climbing, my legs being of little use. My bad leg swung uselessly as I drew myself up from limb to limb and my good leg could only be used as a prop while my hands reached to higher branches.

I was afraid of heights but managed to overcome this by avoiding looking down unless it was necessary.

I could not monkey-climb up a trunk like other boys, but I could climb a rope hand over hand and when the lower limbs were out of my reach Joe would throw a plow-line over one of them and I would pull myself up on this double strand till I could grasp a limb.

When the magpies nested, Joe would stand below yelling a warning just before the birds attacked. I would climb to the limb, swaying in the wind, my face pressed close to the wood, drawing myself slowly along past forks and peeling bark towards the dark, round patch nestling in leaves against the sky and I would hear his yell, "Here she comes!" and I would pause in my climbing, clinging with one arm and waving the other desperately above my head, waiting for the rush of wings, the sharp clack of a snapping bill, and the gust of wind on my face as the magpie lifted and shot skywards again.

If you could watch them making their gliding dive it wasn't so bad because you could strike at them as they came in and they would swerve away with a quick flick of their wings and a furious jab at your hand, but when your back was to them and you needed both hands to hold on with, they often struck you with their bills or wings.

When this happened to me I would hear Joe's voice below, full of quick concern.

"Did he get ya?"

"Yes."

"Where?"

"On the side of the head."

"Is it bleeding?"

"I don't know yet. Wait till I get a grip here."

In a moment when I could free a hand from its grip on the limb I would feel my stinging head then glance at my finger-tips. "She's bleeding," I'd yell to Joe, both pleased and concerned with the evidence.

"Hell! Anyway you haven't got far to go now. About a yard . . . Stretch out now . . . A bit further . . . No . . . To the right a bit . . . Now . . ."

And I would slip a warm egg into my mouth and come down and we would look at it together as it lay on my palm.

Sometimes I fell, but lower limbs generally broke my fall and I was never badly hurt. Once when climbing with Joe, I slipped as I swung for a limb and grabbed Joe's leg instead. Joe tried to kick me loose but I clung to him like a goanna and we both went crashing down through the branches to land clasped together on the bark-strewn ground below, bruised and breathless but intact.

This fall made a big impression on Joe. In moments of reminiscing he would often remark, "I'll never forget the bloody day you grabbed my leg and wouldn't let go. Now what did you do that for? I yelled 'leggo'."

I could never give him a satisfactory answer though I always felt I was justified in clinging to him.

"I dunno," he would say reflectively. "A fellow can't trust you climbing; I'm blowed if he can!"

Joe developed a philosophical attitude towards the falls I had when walking with him. Immediately I plunged forward on my face, or tottered sideways before collapsing, or crashed on my back, Joe would sit down and continue his conversation knowing that, for a little while, I would lie as I fell.

Since I was nearly always tired, a fall offered me an excuse to

E

rest as I lay stretched on the ground, and I would take a twig and search among the grass stems for insects or watch ants hurrying through the tunnels beneath the leaves.

We never mentioned the fall. It didn't seem important. It was part of my walking.

As Joe once remarked, in discussing my falls, "You're not dead; that's the main thing."

If I had a "bad" fall Joe sat down just the same. He never made the mistake of coming to my aid unless I called him. He would sit on the grass, give one glance at me rolling in pain, then look resolutely away and say, "It's a cow!"

In a minute I would lie quietly and Joe would look at me again and say, "What d'ya think? Will we keep going?"

The term he used whenever he mentioned my falls was the term used by bushmen in drought time when their horses and cattle lay dying on the dry earth.

"Another cow went down today," they would say, and Joe would sometimes say to father when father asked him how I was going, "He went down near the creek and then he didn't go down again till we reached the stones."

The big drought that struck Australia at this time introduced Joe and me to fear and pain and suffering we had never known before. In our experience, the world was a pleasant place. The sun was never cruel and God looked after the cows and the horses. When an animal suffered it was because of man; of this we were sure. We often reflected on what we would do if we were a cow or a horse and we always decided we would leap fence after fence until there was only bush around us and no people whatever, and here we would live in perfect happiness till we died peacefully in the shelter of trees with long, green grass to rest upon.

The drought started with the failure of the autumn rains. When the winter rains came the earth was too cold for growth and seeds did not sprout and the perennial grass was eaten down to the roots by hungry cattle. The spring was dry and when summer came in, dust was blowing across paddocks that in other years were covered in grass.

The road stock, horses and cattle, kept by their owners on the three-chain roads that laced the district, wandered for miles looking for feed. They forced themselves through fences into paddocks even barer than the roads they left to pluck a dying shrub or rush.

Farmers, unable to feed those aged horses they had retired to their back paddocks, and lacking the courage to shoot animals they had come to regard as part of their farms, turned them out on to the roads to fend for themselves. They bought badges for them and the weight on their conscience was lifted.

The local Council only permitted stock on the roads when they had, hanging from their necks, a brass badge for which the Council charged five shillings. This badge entitled the purchaser to graze his beast on the road for a year.

On summer nights the jingle of the chains to which these badges were attached, could be heard through the bush as the horses and cattle wearing them came into the road trough to drink.

For miles along the roads branching out from the trough, bands of horses and cattle could be seen muzzling the dusty earth for roots or standing on the metal eating the dry manure left by chaff-fed horses that had been driven by.

Each mob seemed to keep to itself, always going along the same road, always searching the same lanes. As the drought progressed and the burning heat continued, the mobs grew smaller and smaller. Each day the weakest stumbled and fell and the others moved away from the rising dust of its struggling, walking slowly with dragging feet and drooping heads on and on and on till thirst turned them once more and they began the long trek back to the trough.

Along the roads they walked, magpies with gaping bills stood tottering on gum-tree branches, crows flocked across the paddocks cawing and circling as they sighted a dying beast, and over it all from horizon to horizon the haze of bushfire smoke and the smell of burning gum leaves hung disquietingly above the grassless earth.

Each morning the farmers went round their paddocks raising the cattle that were down.

"I lost three more last night," a passing farmer would say to father. "I expect another couple to go down tonight."

Entire herds of dairy cattle died in the rented paddocks of their owners. They lay on their sides, the earth around their hooves kicked into new-moon holes as they struggled to rise.

Day after day under the unclouded sun they kicked and kicked . . . and dust rose above them and floated away. And their heavy breathing could be heard across the paddocks . . . and deep sighs . . . and sometimes a low moaning.

The farmers, hoping for rain, hoping for the miracle that would save them, left the struggling cattle for days. When death had almost come to a cow they killed her with blows then went to the stronger ones who lay lifting their heavy heads and dropping them again; opening wide, staring eyes, struggling to rise.

They placed ropes around them, lifted them with horses, levered them to their feet with planks, held them in an upright position with strong shoulders till the beasts could be left to stand unaided and live another day.

Men leant on gates looking at the blazing sunsets while behind them the empty bails of their cowsheds opened out on to paddocks of bare earth. They gathered round the post office at mail time, talking of their losses and debating how they could raise money to buy hay, how they could hang on till rain came.

Father was having a bad time. He had several of Mrs. Carruthers's horses to break in and she sent down chaff to feed them. Each week Peter Finlay left four bags at our gate and father would take a handful of the chaff and pour it from hand to hand blowing the straw away with his mouth till a little pile of oats lay on his palm. It pleased him when there were a lot of oats. "Good stuff," he would say.

He seemed to spill a lot on the chaff-house floor when he was filling the kerosene tin buckets from the bags. Each evening Joe's father came across with a hearth brush and a bran bag and he swept up all the chaff that was spilt and took it home. He was trying to keep his cow and his horse alive. Chaff was a pound a bag when you could get it and this was his wages for a week so he could not buy it. Joe went into the bush and cut swamp grass but the swamps were dry and soon it was gone.

Joe and I were always talking about the horses we had seen that were down. We tortured ourselves with harrowing descriptions of the slow deaths taking place in the paddocks and bush around us.

For some reason I could not explain, the death of animals in paddocks did not affect either of us as badly as did the death of the road stock. The road stock, it seemed to us, were friendless, deserted, turned out to die, while the cattle and horses in paddocks had owners who felt for them.

On the hot summer evenings when the sky remained red long after the sun had set Joe and I walked down to the road trough to watch the stock come in. The horses came in every second night, being able to survive two days without water. The cattle came in every night but they gradually died round the trough, not being able to range as far as the horses.

One night we sat looking at the sunset and waiting for the horses. The road stretched straight through timber then into open country, disappearing finally over a rise. On the rise were dead gums and these were silhouetted against the red sky in sharp detail. The strongest of winds could not move their dead limbs nor any spring bring leaves upon them. They pointed their skeleton fingers at the red sky, standing as still as death, and in a little while the horses rose from behind the earth on which they stood and moved beneath them, coming towards us with a clinking of neck chains and the clatter of hooves on stones.

They walked down the rise, twenty or more, old and young, their heads drooping, all stumbling a little. As they smelt the water from the distant trough, they raised their heads, gathered themselves and broke into a shambling canter. They did not crowd together as they cantered—one stumbling horse could have brought down several of them and once they were down they never rose again—they cantered apart.

Not one of these horses had lain down for months. Some cantered evenly, some rocked in their stride but they all kept well away from each other.

As the trough came in sight some neighed, others quickened their pace. One bay mare, with hip bones so sharply defined, so prominent, I felt they would surely pierce her dry skin, with each rib showing distinctly on her sides, suddenly faltered in her stride. Her legs crumpled, buckled beneath her . . . she did not stumble and fall; she collapsed, pitching forward a little so that her nose hit the ground before she rolled to her side.

She lay still a moment then made a desperate effort to rise. She rose on to her front legs, struggling to get her hind legs to complete the lift, but they gave way and she fell back on her side once more. As we hurried towards her she raised her head and looked towards the trough. Even when we stood beside her she still looked towards the trough.

"Come on," I cried to Joe. "We've got to raise her. All she wants is a drink and it'll put strength into her. Look at her flanks. She's dry as a bone. Let's get hold of her head."

Joe stood beside me. We placed our hands beneath her neck and tried to lift but she did not move. She was breathing deeply.

"Let her have a blow for a bit," Joe advised. "She might be able to get up then."

We stood beside her in the gathering dark quite unable to accept the fact that she must die. We were restless and nervously irritable with frustration. We wanted to go home but we were afraid to part, for then we would be alone with the tormenting picture of her lying there dying in the night.

I suddenly grabbed her head. Joe slapped her rump. We yelled at her. For a moment she fought to rise then fell back and a shuddering groan came from her as her head sank down to the earth.

We couldn't stand it.

"What the hell is everybody doing?" Joe suddenly shouted angrily, looking round at the empty roads as if expecting strong men with ropes to dash forward to help us.

"We'll have to get her a drink," I said in desperation. "Let's go and get a bucket."

"I'll go," said Joe. "You wait here. Where is it?"

"In the chaff house."

Joe set off running towards our house and I sat down on the ground beside the mare. I could hear mosquitoes and the drone of heavy beetles in flight. Bats ticked above the trees. The rest of the horses had drunk and were slowly filing past me, making back to some far-away spot where some grass butts still lingered. They were like skeletons of horses clothed in skin and I could smell the breath of them as they passed, a smell like musty earth.

When Joe came back with the bucket we filled it at the trough, but it was too heavy for Joe to carry back alone so I helped him. We lifted it a yard at a time. We held the handle together and swung it forward a yard then we would walk ahead of the bucket again and reach back and swing it forward once more until, after repeating this movement a score of times, we reached the mare.

We had heard her neighing her thirst as we got closer to her. When we placed the bucket in front of her she thrust her nose deep into the water and sucked so strongly the level fell swiftly around her nose as we watched it. In a minute she had emptied the bucket. We brought her another one and she emptied that, then another one. . . . But by now I was exhausted. I fell and was too tired to rise. I lay beside the mare, all my strength gone.

"Hell! I'll have to be carting you water next," said Joe.

He sat down beside me looking at the stars and he sat there for a long time not moving or talking. All I could hear was the deep, sad breathing of the horse.

19

ONE Saturday afternoon I stood near the gate and watched Joe running through the timber on his way to our place. He ran in a crouched position with his head tucked between his shoulders and, as he ran, he dodged behind trees and kept looking back as if pursued by bushrangers.

Flinging himself behind an old, redgum tree he lay flat on his stomach, peering from behind the bole towards the trees through which he had just been running. He suddenly flattened himself against the ground like a goanna and I looked and saw Andy running along the track.

Andy didn't dodge behind trees. He ran with an intense purpose that didn't demand concealment.

Joe wriggled in a circle round the tree to keep the trunk between him and Andy, but Andy was familiar with Joe's tactics and went straight to the tree.

Joe rose from behind the trunk and greeted Andy in tones of surprise.

"You, Andy? Cripes, I was just waiting for ya!"

He didn't fool Andy who had exclaimed with great satisfaction, "Got ya!" when Joe appeared.

Joe and I had arranged to meet Skeeter Bronson and Steve McIntyre at the foot of Mt. Turalla. We were taking the dogs, as foxes were often seen amongst the bracken that covered its sides, but our main object was to roll stones down the crater.

The huge rocks we levered from the crater's lip would hurtle down the steep sides of the crater, bounding high in the air, crashing into trees and leaving behind them streaks of torn scrub and fern. When they reached the floor of the crater they were travelling in springing leaps that carried them a little way up the opposite side before they came to rest.

The climb up the mount was an exhausting walk for me. I needed frequent spells that I always had when Joe was my only companion, but when other boys were with us they complained of these stops.

"Cripes! Ya not stoppin' again are ya?"

Sometimes they wouldn't wait and when I finally joined them at the top, the quick triumph of that first bound over the crest had gone and exclamations of excitement were finished.

I stole time for resting by claiming the attention of those with me. I would point to runs through the ferns and exclaim, "I can smell a fox! He musta just passed! Follow him up, Joe!"

The discussion as to whether it was worth following the trail took time, and I would gain the rest I needed.

Skeeter and Steve were kneeling beside a rabbit burrow when we arrived at the clump of wattle where we were to meet them. They were looking at the tail and hindquarters of Tiny, an Australian terrier owned by Skeeter. Tiny's head, shoulders and front legs were submerged in the burrow and he was scratching vigorously.

"Did ya see any go in?" demanded Joe who had dropped to his knees in front of them with the authoritative air of the expert. "Here! Give me a go!" He grabbed Tiny's hind legs.

"Pull him out and we'll feel down the burra," I said, equally as efficient as Joe.

"Any bloke who puts his hand down a burra is a fool," said Steve rising to his feet and brushing his knees as if his interest in the burrow was now at an end. He had never forgiven me for my victory in our fight with sticks.

"Who's frightened of snakes!" I exclaimed contemptuously, lying on my side and thrusting my arm up the burrow while Joe held the struggling Tiny.

"Ya can feel the end of it," I announced scornfully after wriggling my shoulder deeper into the burrow's mouth.

"It's a breedin' burra," said Joe. He released Tiny who again dived into the burrow as I removed my arm. With the stump of his tail rigidly still he gave three long, investigating sniffs then backed out and looked up at us questioningly.

"Come on," said Steve. "Let's get goin'."

"Where's Andy?" asked Joe. Andy was sitting on the ground between Dummy and Rover. He had been parting Rover's hair looking for fleas, an operation that Rover bore with a still, entranced expression on his lifted face.

"What did ya bring Andy for?" asked Skeeter with an expression of suffering on his face.

Andy looked quickly at Joe for a satisfactory explanation of his presence.

"Because I brought him, that's why," replied Joe truculently. Joe never wasted any time on Skeeter. "I'd punch him as soon as look at him," was a frequent remark of his which expressed his opinion of Skeeter.

We followed a narrow horse-pad that girdled the side of the hill. It was a difficult path for me. The ferns that skirted it were high and offered stiff, tangling resistance to each swing of my crutches. Wide tracks presented no such problems and I always looked for them when I walked through the bush, but on Mt. Turalla the tracks were all narrow pads, hip-high in fern. I kept one chutch swinging along the open pathway, my legs and the other crutch forcing their way through the growth.

I never considered my legs; a passageway for them was unnecessary. My weight only rested on my good leg for an instant before both legs swung forward again, but the state of the ground upon which my crutches rested, the obstructions opposing them, were important. A fall always came from a slipping crutch, or the striking of its tip on a stone, or its entanglement in grass or fern, never from the failure of my legs to complete their swing.

When Joe first began walking with me it worried him to see my legs bashing their way through ferns while an unobstructed track ran beside me. The movement of one crutch along this pathway seemed unimportant to him; it was the course my legs followed that was the measure of my comfort in his eyes and he often complained, "Why don't you walk on the track where it's easy?"

After I explained it to him he remarked, "It's a beggar, isn't it!" then never mentioned it again.

The strategy I used to distract Skeeter and Steve from their intention to reach the top without delay succeeded, and we all walked over the crest together. The unimpeded wind blew strongly against us and we breasted it with delight, sending loud yells echoing round the crater lying like a deep bowl in front of us.

We sent a rock bounding down its steep slopes, watching the falling flight of the stone with excitement. I longed to follow it, to see for myself what lay hidden down there amongst the ferns and trees that grew on the bottom.

"They reckon there might be a big hole down there with just a bit of earth covering it," I said, "and if you stood on it—hell! you'd go through into boiling mud and everything."

"It's extinct," said Steve with a typical lack of co-operation.

"It might be," Joe argued aggressively, "but just as like as not the whole bottom's sorta soft and ready to fall in. There's no knowin' what's down there," he ended solemnly. "By cripes, there's not!"

"I'll bet Blacks lived down there once," said Skeeter. "You'd see where they'd been if you went down. Mr. Tucker found a Blackfellow's axe up here."

"That's nothin'," said Joe. "I know a bloke's got half a dozen."

"I'm going half-way down," said Steve.

"Come on!" said Skeeter eagerly. "It'll be good fun. I'll go. Come on, Joe."

Joe looked at me. "I'll wait for you," I said.

The slopes of the crater were littered with scoria and stones that long ago must have bubbled in some fierce heat before solidifying. They were lumps of froth turned into stone and they were so light they floated on water. There were outcrops of rocks with the smooth surface of an arrested liquid and round stones with cores of green gravel. Odd gum trees grew on the steep sides and there were large patches of bracken.

My crutches would not grip on this steep, crumbling earth and even where the tips rested firm it was impossible to leap down so steep a slope. I sat down with my crutches lying beside me, prepared to wait till they returned.

Andy was determined to go with Joe on this adventure.

"I can't go far with Andy." Joe was making it easy for me. "He'd knock up if we went to the bottom. I'll go half-way down."

"I can walk like anything," protested Andy, anxious to reassure Joe.

"We won't be long," Joe assured me.

133

I watched them moving downward, Joe holding Andy by the hand. Their voices got further away till I could not hear them.

It did not distress me that I could not go with them. I believed I was staying because of my decision to stay and not because of my helplessness. I *never* felt helpless. I was exasperated, but my exasperation did not arise from my inability to walk and climb like Joe or Steve; it was directed against the Other Boy.

The Other Boy was always with me. He was my shadow-self, weak and full of complaints, afraid and apprehensive, always pleading with me to consider him, always seeking to restrain me for his own selfish interests. I despised him, yet he was my responsibility. In all moments of decision I had to free myself of his influence. I argued with him then, when he would not be convinced; I spurned him in fury and went my way. He wore my body and walked on crutches. I strode apart from him on legs as strong as trees.

When Joe had announced he was going to walk down the crater, the Other Boy spoke quickly to me in urgent tones: "Give me a go, Alan. Go easy. I've had enough. Don't make me tired. Stop with me a little while till I get my wind. I won't try and stop you next time."

"All right," I assured him, "but don't come at that too often or I'll leave you. There are a lot of things I want to do and you're not going to stop me from doing them."

So the two of us sat there on the hillside, the one confident of his ability to do all that was asked of him, the other dependent on the first one's patronage and care.

It was a quarter of a mile to the bottom of the crater. I could see the boys scrambling down the slope, moving now to the right or the left seeking easier places or holding on to the trunk of a tree while they stood a moment looking around them.

I expected them to turn at any moment and come climbing back again. When I saw they had made up their minds to continue to the bottom I felt a sense of betrayal and muttered to myself in annoyance.

I looked at my crutches for a moment, wondering whether they would be safe there and if I could remember where I left them; then I turned on to my hands and knees and set off for the bottom where the boys were now calling to each other and exploring the flat area they had reached.

At first I crawled, crashing my way through ferns with little effort as I went plunging downward. Sometimes my hands slipped and I fell on my face, skidding on loose earth till I was stopped by some obstruction. On areas of scoria I sat upright as in a sled and went sliding down for yards amid a cascade of gravel and bouncing pebbles.

Near the bottom the huge stones that once had rested on the top of the mount lay in piled confusion among the fern. Ever since the early pioneers had entered this country those who climbed the mount had been levering these heavy rocks from where they had been lying half-buried on the summit, and had watched them hurtling downwards till they rolled to a stop far below.

I found it difficult to cross this barrier of tumbled stone. I moved from rock to rock, taking all my weight on my hands to save my knees, but when I at length reached a less crowded area where I could crawl between them, my knees were scratched and bleeding.

The boys had watched me coming down and when I came tumbling through a belt of fern on to level ground, Joe and Andy were waiting for me.

"How in the hell are ya goin' to get up?" Joe asked as he dropped down on the grass beside me. "It must be after three o'clock now and I've got to bring the ducks home."

"I'll get up easy," I told him shortly, then continued in a change of tone, "Is the ground soft down here like what you thought? Let's roll over stones and see what's underneath 'em."

"It's just like on top," said Joe. "Skeeter caught a lizard but he won't let you hold it. Steve and 'im keep talking about us when I'm not there. Look at 'em now."

Skeeter and Steve were standing near a tree talking and glancing towards us with the unmistakable furtiveness of conspirators.

"We can hear you," I yelled out. This lie was the traditional opening to acknowledgments of enmity and Steve replied with undisguised hostility. "Who're *you* talking to?" he demanded, taking a step towards us.

"Not to you, anyway," called Joe who regarded this answer

as a devastating retort. He turned to me grinning happily, "Didja hear me give it to him?"

"Look, they're off," I said. Skeeter and Steve had turned and were beginning the climb up the side of the crater. "Let 'em go. Who cares for them?"

Skeeter looked back over his shoulder and shouted a final insult. "Both of youse are cranky."

Joe and I were disappointed at the poor quality of this thrust. It was too uninspiring to rouse a spirited reply and we watched the two boys in silence as they picked their way through the stones.

"Skeeter couldn't fight his way out of a paper bag," Joe asserted.

"I could, couldn't I, Joe?" piped Andy. Andy's estimate of his ability was always based on Joe's opinion.

"Yes," said Joe. He chewed a grass stem then said to me, "We'd better get goin'. I gotta get the ducks yet."

"All right," I said, then added, "You needn't wait for me less you like. I'll be jake."

"Come on," said Joe rising.

"Wait till I just feel I'm down here," I said.

"It seems funny, don't it," said Joe looking round. "Listen to how it echoes."

"Hullo!" he yelled and round the side of the crater came faint "Hullos" in answer to him.

For a little while we sent echoes tumbling from the slopes then Joe said, "Let's go. I don't like down here."

"Why don't you, Joe?" asked Andy.

"It's like as if it'll fall in on you," he said.

"It won't fall in, will it, Joe?" asked Andy anxiously.

"No," said Joe. "I'm only talkin'."

Yet it did seem as if the enclosing sides would topple over and down, shutting us off from the sky. From here the sky was no longer a dome that covered the earth but a frail roof resting on walls of stone and gravel. It was pale and thin, drained of its familiar blue and rendered insignificant by the mighty slopes that rose to meet it.

And the earth was brown, brown . . . All brown . . . The dark green of the ferns was swamped with brown. The still, silent boulders were brown. Even the silence was brown. We sat cut off from the bright sounds of the living world that lay over the encircling rim and all the while we felt we were being watched by something huge and unfriendly.

"We'll go," I said, after a silence. "It feels crook down here."

I lowered myself on to the earth from the stone on which I had been sitting.

"No one will ever believe I've been down here," I said.

"It just shows what fools they are," said Joe.

I turned and began crawling back. In crawling up a steep slope the weight is thrown on to the knees and mine were already inflamed and tender. Coming down, my arms had taken my weight and no power had been demanded of my knees that merely supported me. Now I had to struggle with each yard I traversed and I quickly tired. I had to rest every few yards, sinking down with my face pressed to the ground and my arms lying limp beside me. In this position I could hear the beating of my heart coming from the earth.

When I rested Joe and Andy sat each side of me and talked but after a while we climbed and rested in silence, each occupied with his own problems. Joe had to help Andy, at the same time keeping pace with me.

I crawled on and on exhorting myself with silent commands to greater endeavour. "Now!" "Again!" "This time!"

High up on the crater's side we stopped for one of our rests. I lay full length on the earth breathing deeply and from the ground against which my ear was pressed I heard two quick thuds. I looked up towards the top of the crater and there outlined against the sky were Skeeter and Steve and they were yelling in fear and waving their arms.

"Look out! Look out!"

The stone that under a sudden impulse they had sent rolling down on us had not yet gathered speed. Joe saw it at the same time as I did.

"The tree," he yelled. He grabbed Andy and the three of us floundered towards an old dead gum that towered from the crater's side. We reached it just before the stone passed us with a shrill whistle and thuds that shook the ground. We watched it leaping wildly over ferns and logs away below us and then heard the sharp crack as it struck the boulders hidden in bracken. It broke in half and the two pieces separated and shot away from each other at an angle.

Steve and Skeeter, frightened by what they had done, had turned and were running over the crest.

"They're gone!" I said.

"Cripes! Didja ever see the like!" said Joe. "They mighta killed us."

But we both felt pleased that this had happened to us.

"Wait till we tell the kids at school," I said.

We began our climb again feeling a little better and talking about the speed of the stone but soon we were silent again and when I rested Joe and Andy just sat there looking back at the crater below us.

It seemed to me we were all struggling together and their silence, like mine, was that of exhaustion.

I began spelling more frequently and when the sun was beginning to set and the sky was flaming red behind the opposite crest I had to sink to the ground after each painful, forward heave.

When finally we reached the top I lay on the ground while all my flesh twitched like that of a kangaroo from which the hide had just been taken.

Joe sat beside me holding my crutches and in a little while he said, "I'm getting worried over those ducks."

I rose to my feet, placed the crutches beneath my arms, and we set off down the mountain.

20

It troubled father to see me returning exhausted from long walks in the bush. One day he said, "Don't walk so far, Alan. Hunt in the bush round the house."

"There are no hares there," I said.

"No." He stood looking at the ground and thinking. "You've got to hunt, have you?" he asked me.

"No," I said, "but I like going out hunting. All the boys go hunting. I like going out with Joe. He stops when I'm tired."

"Yes, Joe's a good bloke," father reflected.

"Getting tired's nothing," I said to him when he remained silent.

"No, that's true enough. I suppose you'll have to have a crack at the lot. Anyway, toss it in and lie down when you're done. You might have a champion horse but you've still got to spell him going up a long hill."

He saved some money and began looking at the second-hand advertisements in the *Age*. One day he wrote a letter and a few weeks later he drove to Balunga and brought home an invalid chair that came up in the train.

It was standing in the yard when I came home from school and I stood looking at it in amazement. Father yelled out from the stockyard, "It's yours. Hop into the saddle and give it a fly."

The chair was a heavy, cumbersome affair built with no regard to saving weight. It had two over-size bicycle wheels at the back and a small wheel in the front attached to the frame by a cast goose-neck. Two long handles, one each side of the seat, were attached to rods that were fitted to cranks on the axle. The handles were worked to and fro, one going forward as the other came back. The right handle had a swivel attachment that enabled the rider to turn the front wheel to the right or left.

It took a heavy pull to start it moving but once it was in motion it could be kept moving by a rhythmic working of the arms.

I climbed into it and rode it round the yard in a series of jerky, forward movements, but after a while I learned to relax momentarily at the end of each sweep so that it ran smoothly along like a bicycle.

After a few days I could race it up the road, my arms working like pistons. I rode it to school and became the envy of my mates who climbed aboard with me, either sitting on my knee or facing one another sitting on the goose-neck. The one in front could grasp the handles lower down than my grip and help work them to and fro. We called it "working your passage" and I would give anybody a lift who worked his passage.

However, those who sat in front, not having arms trained to thrusting on crutches, soon tired and I was left to work the handles without help.

The invalid chair extended my range of movement and brought the creek within reach. Turalla Creek was three miles away from our home and I only saw it on Sunday School picnic days or when father drove that way in the brake.

Joe often walked to the creek to fish for eels and now I could accompany him. We tied our two bamboo rods beside the seat, placed a sugar bag on the footboard for carrying the eels, and set off with Joe sitting in front working his arms with short, swift strokes while high up on the handles my arms worked with longer sweeps.

Saturday night was our fishing night and we always left home in the late afternoon, arriving at McCallum's Hole before the sun set. McCallum's Hole was a long, dark stretch of water, deep and still. Redgums lined its banks and threw powerful limbs across the water. Their trunks were gnarled and twisted, charred by bush fires or bearing the long, leaf-like scar left by a Blackfellow after he had removed the bark for a canoe.

Joe and I fashioned stories around these canoe trees which we examined eagerly, looking for the marks of the stone axe that had been used to cut the bark from the trunk. Some of the

140

scars were small, no longer than a child, and we knew the bark from these had been used to fashion coolamons, the shallow dish in which the lubras placed their piccaninnies to sleep or in which they carried the vegetable food they gathered.

One such tree grew with its huge, coiling roots touched by the water of McCallum's Hole. On still nights when our floaters sat motionlessly in a moonlight path on the water, the dark surface at our feet would glitter with ripples then break and for a moment a platypus would be floating there, watching us with sharp eyes before it curved its body and returned to its burrow amongst the submerged roots of the old tree.

They used to swim upriver against the current then float back, their heads still facing the stream as they searched for worms and grubs the current was carrying. Sometimes we thought they were fish as they floated by with only their curved backs above the surface and we would cast our lines towards them. If one took the bait we pulled it out on to the bank where we touched its fur and talked about how we would like to keep it, before we let it go.

Water rats also lived in holes beneath the tree. They brought up mussels from the mud below and broke the shells on the flat surface of one huge root from where we gathered the pieces and put them in a bag to bring home to the fowls.

"It's the best shell grit you can get," Joe told me, but Joe always dealt in superlatives. He described my invalid chair as "the best made thing he had ever seen" and wondered why they never had races for them.

"You'd be a champion, easy," Joe assured me. "Now, say you were on scratch. . . Well, that wouldn't matter a beggar. No other bloke's got arms like you. You'd romp it in."

He talked like this while we sat facing each other on the chair, our arms moving rhythmically to and fro as we made for the creek. We both felt very happy on this night for we had made a "bob".

Catching eels with a hook can be exciting but with a bob the excitement is continuous and the catch much bigger.

A bob is made by threading worms on to a strand of wool till you have one tremendous worm several yards long.

This heavy worm-string is then looped into a drooping bunch to which the line is tied. It is not used with a float. It is cast into the water as it is, where it sinks to the bottom and is almost immediately seized by an eel whose file-like teeth get caught in the wool.

When the one holding the line feels the tug he jerks the eel from the water and it falls with the bob on to the bank beside him. He then has to seize it before it escapes back into the water, cut through the back of its neck with a knife and thrust it into his bag.

Eels are slimy and are hard to hold and sometimes two would be jerked to the bank at once and Joe and I would dive after them, grabbing them and losing them, then flinging ourselves upon them again. While we were waiting for a bite we rubbed the palms of our hands on the dry earth so that the dust adhering there would prevent our grip from slipping. The slime from the eels caked this dirt and after a while we had to wash it off then rub them in the dust again.

We lit a campfire when we reached the old tree and boiled the billy into which mother had already placed the tea and sugar. We watched flocks of ducks come swiftly up the creek, following each bend and rising steeply when they saw us.

"There's a power of ducks on this creek," Joe said munching a thick corned beef sandwich. "I'd like a penny for every duck, say, from here to Turalla."

"How much do you reckon you'd have?" I asked him.

"A hundred pound, easy," said Joe who always argued in round figures.

Joe regarded a hundred pounds as a fortune. "You never know what you could do with a hundred quid," he told me. "You could do anything."

This was an absorbing subject.

"You could buy any pony you wanted," I said. "Buckjump saddles!—Cripes! Say you wanted to buy a book, now. . . . Well, you could get it and if you lent it to anybody and they wouldn't give it back, it wouldn't matter."

"Aw, you'd easy get it back," Joe said. "You'd know who had it."

"You mightn't," I insisted. "No one remembers who they lend books to."

I threw my crusts into the river and Joe said, "Don't frighten hell outa the eels. Eels is terrible nervous and, what's more, there's an east wind tonight and they won't bite with an east wind."

He stood up and wet his finger by thrusting it into his mouth. He held it upright in the still air and waited a moment.

"Yes, it's east all right. It feels cold on the east side."

But the eels bit better than Joe anticipated. I had no sooner lifted the bob from the grass-lined tin in which we kept it and cast it into the water than I felt a bite on the line. I jerked the rod upwards and flung the bob with an eel attached on to the bank. The eel floundered on the grass then wriggled towards the water like a snake.

"Grab it!" I yelled. Joe grabbed it and held it squirming in his hands while I opened the pocket knife. I severed its backbone behind its neck and we placed it in the sugar bag which we put down beside the fire.

"That's one," said Joe with satisfaction. "The east wind musta died down—a good job, too. We'll get a lot tonight."

By eleven o'clock we had eight eels, but Joe wanted ten.

"When ya got ten it makes out ya good," he reasoned. "It's better to say, 'we got ten last night' than to say 'we got eight'."

We decided to stay till twelve o'clock. The moon had risen and there was plenty of light to see our way home. Joe gathered more wood for the fire. It was cold and we were thinly clad.

"You can't beat a good fire," I said, throwing dry gum branches into the flames till they billowed up higher than our heads.

Joe dropped an armful of wood and ran to grab the rod which had moved to the tug of an eel. He flung the eel out on to the bank where it fell near the fire, glittering with black and silver as it writhed away from the heat.

It was the biggest eel we had caught and I flung myself at it eagerly. It slipped from my grasp and slithered towards the water. I rubbed my hands desperately on the ground and crawled after it but Joe had dropped the rod and had seized it near the edge of the water. It wriggled in his hands, threshing its head and tail. Joe gripped it tenaciously but it squeezed through his hands and fell to the ground. He dived at it again as it was entering the water but he slipped on the mud and went into the creek up to his waist.

Joe never swore much but he swore now. It was funny to see

him in the water but I didn't laugh. He crawled out on to the bank and stood up, his arms curved away from his sides as he looked down at the pool of water gathering at his feet.

"I'll get into a row over this," he said in a tone of concern. "By hell, I will! I'll have to dry my pants if it's the last thing I do."

"Take 'em off and dry 'em at the fire," I suggested. "They won't take long. How did he get away from you?"

Joe looked back at the creek. "That eel was the biggest eel I've ever seen in me life," he said. "I couldn't get me hands round it. And heavy!—Cripes, it was heavy! Did ya feel the weight of it?"

Here was a wonderful opportunity for creating an experience that could never be checked and Joe and I revelled in it.

"It felt like a ton," I said.

"Easy," Joe reckoned.

"What about the way it lashed round," I exclaimed. "You could feel it fighting like a snake."

"It got round me arm," said Joe, "and I thought it was broke." He paused then began taking off his trousers with great speed as if a bull ant had gone up his leg. "I gotta get these dry."

I thrust the end of a forked stick into the ground so that it leant almost over the fire where his trousers would dry quickly in the rising heat.

Joe took a piece of sodden string, a brass door knob and some marbles from his pocket and placed them on the ground, then he hung his trousers on the stick and began dancing up and down before the fire to keep warm.

I flung the bob back into the creek, hoping to catch the eel we had lost and when I finally felt a bite I jerked the rod with the power of one about to lift a heavy weight.

A wriggling eel, clinging to the bob, flashed high in the air above my head, came down in a curve behind me, and crashed into the stick holding Joe's trousers. The trousers fell into the fire.

Joe dived towards the fire then backed precipitately as a flare of heat burst against his face. He raised one hand to shield his face and tried to reach his trousers with the other. He suddenly raced round the fire swearing in an anguished fashion then grabbed the rod from my hands and poked at his flaming trousers in an effort to hook them and jerk them out. When at length he got the end of the rod beneath them, he was desperate for time and he gave such a tremendous heave on the rod that the trousers leaped upwards from the flames and described a rainbow of fire against the night before sailing on free of the rod and dropping with a sizzle and a puff of steam into the waters of the creek.

As the flames were extinguished a great darkness came upon Joe. The black patch of his sinking trousers could be seen against the gleam of the moving water before they disappeared, and he watched this patch, bending out over the water with his hands on his knees and the glow of the fire painting his bare behind a rosy pink.

"My God!" he said.

When he had recovered sufficiently to discuss his predicament he announced that we must get home quickly. He had lost interest in catching ten eels and was concerned over being seen without trousers.

"It's agin the law to leave your pants off," he told me earnestly. "If any bloke seen me without pants I'd be done. You can do a stretch quick and lively if you're caught without pants. Old Dobson," Joe was referring to a local racing cyclist who had recently gone off his head, "went to Melbourne and ran clean through it without pants an' they jailed him for hell only knows how long. We gotta get going. I wish it wasn't a full moon."

We hurriedly tied our rods to the side of the chair, placed the bag of eels on the footboard and set off, Joe sitting on my knee in gloomy silence.

I had a heavy load and when we came to a hill Joe had to get out and push. But there were not many hills and I got slower and slower.

Joe complained of the cold. My exertions on the handles kept me warm and I was protected from the breeze of our passage by Joe who kept slapping his bare thighs to warm them.

Far ahead of us, on a long, straight stretch of road, we saw the lights of a buggy approaching us. We could hear the clock-clock of a jogging horse and I said, "That sounds like old O'Connor's grey."

"That'll be him," said Joe. "Pull up! You never know who'll

145

be with him. Let me off. I'll hide behind the trees over there. He'll think you're on your own."

I stopped the chair on the side of the road and Joe ran across the grass and disappeared into a dark clump of trees.

I sat there watching the approaching buggy, glad of the rest, and thinking of each section of the road ahead of me—the easy parts, the long rises, our lane and the last pull home.

When the candle lamps of the buggy were still a little way off the driver pulled his horse to a walk and when he came level with my chair he called out, "Whoa," and the horse stopped. He leant forward in the seat and peered at me.

"Goodday, Alan."

"Goodnight, Mr. O'Connor."

He looped the reins over his arm and felt for his pipe.

"Where you off to?"

"I've been fishing," I told him.

"Fishing!" he exclaimed. "Strewth!" He ground tobacco between his palms and murmured, "It beats me what a kid like you wants to go round ridin' in that bloody contraption in the middle of the night for. You'll go and get yourself kilt. Look, I'm tellin' ya!" He raised his voice, "You'll get bloody well run over be someone who's boozed—that's what'll happen to you."

He leant over the mudguard and spat on the ground.

"I'm damned if I can make your old man out and there's a lot more can't make him out either. A kid crippled up like you should be home restin' in bed." He shrugged resignedly. "Well, it's nothin' to do with me I suppose, praise God! Have you got a match on you, now?"

I climbed from the chair, untied my crutches from beside the seat and handed him a box. He struck a match and held it to his pipe. He sucked vigorously with a gurgling noise as the flame rose and fell above the bowl. He handed me the box then raised his head with the pipe projecting upwards at an angle and continued drawing on it until a sudden glow came from the bowl.

"Yes," he said, "we all have our troubles. Here's me with the rheumatiz in me shoulder somethin' terrible. I know what it is. . . ." He gathered in the reins then paused and asked "How's your old man goin' these days?"

146

"Pretty good," I answered, "he's breaking five of Mrs. Carruthers's."

"Her!" snorted Mr. O'Connor. "Hell!" then added, "Ask him if he'll handle a three-year-old filly I've got. She's broken to lead. Quiet as a lamb too. . . . How much does he charge?"

"Thirty bob," I said.

"Too much," he said firmly. "I'll give him a quid—an' a good price too. She hasn't got a buck in her. You ask him."

"All right," I promised.

He pulled on the reins. "I'm damned if I know what a kid like you goes round in the middle of the bloody night for," he muttered. "Giddup."

His horse roused itself and moved off.

"Hurroo," he said.

"Goodnight, Mr. O'Connor."

When he had gone Joe emerged from the clump of trees and came running over to the chair.

"I'm frozen stiff," he muttered impatiently. "If I bent me legs I'd crack 'em. What did he stop so long for? Quick, let's get goin'."

He clambered on to my knee and we set off again, Joe shivering convulsively between exclamations of concern and anger at the loss of his trousers.

"Mum'll go stone mad. I've only got one other pair and the backside's out of 'em."

I pulled and pushed at the handles with all my strength, my forehead pressed hard against Joe's back. The chair bounced along over the rough road with the long rods clacking together and the eels slipping from side to side in the bag at our feet.

"One thing," said Joe seeking to comfort himself, "I took everything out of the pockets of me pants before they were burnt."

21

A SWAGMAN sitting near our gate had told me he knew a man who had both legs off and yet he could swim like a fish. I often thought of this man swimming like a fish in the water. I had never seen anyone swimming and I had no idea how you moved your arms to keep afloat.

I had a large, bound volume of a boys' paper called *Chums* in which there was an article on swimming. It was illustrated with three pictures of a man in a striped bathing suit and a moustache who, in the first picture, stood facing you with his arms stretched above his head; the next picture showed his arms stretched out at right angles to his body, and in the last picture they were by his side. Arrows curving from his hands to his knees suggested he moved his arm downward in what the writer called the "Breast Stroke", a name that was faintly distasteful to me since I always associated the word "breast" with a mother feeding her baby.

The article mentioned that a frog used the breast stroke when swimming and I caught some frogs and put them in a bucket of water. They swam to the bottom, circled it then came up again and floated with their noses on the surface and their legs widespread and still each side of them. I did not learn very much from watching them but I was determined to learn to swim and on summer evenings began sneaking off in my chair to a lake three miles away where I began practising.

The lake lay hidden in a hollow with the steep, high bank rising in terraces for two or three hundred yards from the water. These terraces must have continued beneath the surface, for a few yards out from the edge the bottom dropped abruptly into depths where trailing waterweeds grew and the water was cold and still.

148

None of the boys at the school could swim nor could any of the men I knew in Turalla. There were no suitable bathing places in the district and only on very hot evenings, and under a strong incentive, were men tempted to go to the lake which was always regarded as dangerous. Children were warned to keep away from it.

However, groups of boys sometimes ignored their parents' instructions and splashed in the water round the edge trying to teach themselves to swim. If any men were present at these times they kept their eyes on me and wouldn't let me go close to the "holes", as we called the place where the bed dropped away to deep water. They carried me from the bank to the shallow section, being concerned if they saw me crawling across the stones and through the belt of mud that skirted the edge.

"Here, I'll give you a lift!" they would say.

They concentrated the attention of all who were there upon me. When no men were present the boys never seemed aware that I crawled when they walked. They splashed water on me, plastered me with mud in our mud fights, or fell upon me and pummelled me with wet fists.

In our fights with mud I was a perfect target since I could not dodge or pursue the one who attacked me. I could easily have withdrawn from such battles; I could have called out "barley" and given them the victory. But if I had done these things I would never have been able to preserve an equality with them. I would always have been an onlooker, the victim of an attitude they reserved for girls.

I was never conscious of any reasoning behind my actions nor was I aware that I was directed by motives designed to give me equality. I acted under compulsions I did not recognise and could not explain. Thus, when faced with a determined boy throwing mud at me, I crawled straight towards him, disregarding every handful he hurled, till finally, when I was about to grapple with him, he would turn and flee.

It was so in fights with sticks. I moved straight into the fray and took the blows, for only in this way could I earn the respect given by children to those who excelled at games.

Swimming was an achievement upon which the children placed great value and it was the custom to proclaim you could swim when you could lie face downwards upon the water and draw yourself forward with your hands on the bottom. But I wanted to be able to swim in deep water and since other children so rarely went to the lake I began going out there alone.

I left my chair in a wattle clump on the top of the bank then scrambled down the grass-covered terraces till I reached the shore where I undressed and crawled across the stones and mud till I reached the sand. Here I could sit down with the water no higher than my chest.

The article in *Chums* said nothing about bending your arms and thrusting them forward in a way that offered no resistance to the water. My interpretation of the drawings was that you merely moved your straightened arms up and down.

I reached the stage where I could keep myself afloat with a mighty threshing but could not go forward and it was not till the second year, when I discussed swimming with another swagman at our gate, that I learned how to move my arms.

I learned very quickly after that until there came a day when I felt I could swim anywhere. I decided to test myself out over the "holes".

It was a hot summer evening and the lake was as blue as the sky. I sat naked on the bank watching the black swans far out on the water, rising and falling as they rode the tiny waves, while I argued with the Other Boy who wanted me to go home.

"You swam easily a hundred yards along the edge," he reasoned. "No other boy at school could do that."

But I would not listen to him until he said, "See how lonely it is."

It was the loneliness that frightened me. No trees grew around this lake. It lay open to the sky and there was always a still silence above it. Sometimes a swan called out but it was a mournful cry and only accentuated the lake's isolation.

After a while I crawled into the water and continued on, keeping erect by moving my arms in a swimming stroke on the surface, till I reached the edge of the drop into the dark blue and the cold. I stood there moving my arms and looking down into the clear water where I could see the long, pale stems of weeds swaying like snakes as they stretched out from the steep side of the submerged terrace.

150

I looked up at the sky and it was immense above me, an empty dome of sky with a floor of blue water. I was alone in the world and I was afraid.

I stood there a little while then drew a breath and struck out over the drop. As I moved forward a cold tendril of leaves clung for a moment to my trailing legs then slipped away and I was swimming in water that I felt went down beneath me for ever.

I wanted to turn back but I kept on, moving my arms with a slow rhythm while I kept repeating over and over in my mind, "Don't be frightened now; don't be frightened now; don't be frightened now."

I turned gradually and when I was facing the shore again and saw how far away it seemed to be I panicked for a moment and churned up the water with my arms, but the voice within me kept on and I recovered myself and swam slowly again.

I crawled out on to the shore as if I were an explorer returning home from a long journey of danger and privation. The lakeside was now no longer a lonely place of fear but a very lovely place of sunshine and grass and I whistled as I dressed.

I could swim!

22

Our gateway was shaded by huge redgums. The scattered charcoal of campfires lay amongst the leaves, twigs and branches that littered the ground beneath them. Swagmen passing along the road often slipped their swags off their shoulders and rested here or stood looking speculatively at the house and the wood heap before coming in to beg some tucker.

Mother was well known to those swaggies whose beat passed our home. She always gave them bread, meat and tea without asking them to chop wood in return.

Father had humped his bluey in Queensland and was familiar with the ways of swagmen. He always called them "travellers". The bearded men who kept to the bush he called "Scrub Turkeys" and those who came down from the plains he called "Plain Turkeys". He could tell the difference between them and whether they were broke or not.

When a swaggie camped at our gate for the night father always said he was broke.

"If he were holding well, he'd keep on to the pub," he told me.

From the stockyard he often watched them carrying billies to our door and if they clung to the lid of the billy and didn't hand it to mother he would smile and say "old-timer".

I asked him what it meant when they held on to the lid while mother took the billy and he said, "When you're on the track there's some people as wouldn't give you the smell of an oilrag. You've gotta work 'em along like you was a sheep dog. Say, now, you want tea and sugar—that's what you always want. You put a few leaves of tea in the bottom of the billy—not many, enough so she knows you're light on the tea. When she comes to the door you don't ask for tea. What you ask for is a drop of hot water to make some tea and you say 'The tea's in the billy, lady.' She takes the billy and you hang on to the lid, then you say, as if you'd just thought of it see, 'You could stick in a bit of sugar if you don't mind, lady!'

"Now when she goes to put the hot water in the billy she sees there's not enough tea in it to colour a spit so she chucks in some more. She mightn't want to but she don't like handing it back to a bloke weak as dishwater so she shoves in more tea. Then she chucks in the sugar and he's got the lot."

"But why does he hold on to the lid?" I persisted.

"Well, you never get as much if they can cover it up. When there's no lid to hide what they give you they don't like facing you unless the billy is full."

"Mum's not like that, is she, dad?"

"Hell, no!" he said. "She'd give you the boots off her feet if you let her."

"Has she ever?" I asked, interested in the picture of mother taking off her boots and giving them to a swagman.

"Aw, well . . . No, if it comes to that. She could give them old clothes or boots but anybody'd give them clothes. It's tucker they want, especially meat. Giving tucker costs money. A lot of people 'd sooner give 'em a pair of old pants their old man won't wear no more. You give them meat when you grow up."

Sometimes a swagman slept in our chaff house. Mary was feeding the ducks one frosty morning and she saw a swaggie covered in a blanket as stiff as a board. He had frost on his beard and eyebrows and when he got up he walked round in a stooped position till the sun warmed him.

After that, when Mary saw a swagman camped at the gate, she sent me down to tell him he could sleep in the chaff house. I always followed him into the chaff house and when mother sent Mary out with his dinner she would send me out my dinner too. She knew I liked swagmen. I liked to hear them talking and hear about the wonderful places they had seen. Father said they pulled my leg but I didn't think so.

When I showed one old man my rabbit skins, he told me that where he came from the rabbits were so thick you had to sweep them aside to set the traps.

It was a dusty night and I told him if he put the *Age* over his face it would keep the dust off him. I slept out on the back verandah and I always did it.

"How much dust would it keep off?" he asked me as he raised a black billy to his mouth. "Would it keep off a pound of dust now?"

"I think so," I said doubtfully.

"Do you think it would keep off a ton of dust?" he asked, wiping drops of tea from his moustache and beard with the back of his hand.

"No," I said, "it wouldn't."

"I been crossing outback stations where you got to sleep with a pick and shovel beside you when a dust storm's coming on."

"What for?" I asked.

"So's you can dig yourself out' in the morning," he said, looking at me with his strange little black eyes that had lights in them.

I always believed everything I was told and it troubled me when father laughed at the stories I repeated to him. I felt it showed he was criticising the man who had told me.

"It's not that at all; I like the blokes that tell 'em," he explained, "but they're fairy stories, see; funny fairy stories that make you laugh."

Sometimes a swaggie would sit over his campfire and shout at the trees or mumble to himself as he looked at the flames; then I knew he was drunk. Sometimes he would be drinking wine and sometimes methylated spirits.

There was a man called "The Fiddler" who always held his

head a little to one side as if he were playing a fiddle. He was tall and thin and was a three-strap man.

Father had told me that one strap round the swag meant a newchum who had never been on the track before; two straps meant you were looking for work; three straps showed you didn't want to find it; and four straps was a travelling delegate.

I always looked at the straps on their swags and when I saw the three straps on The Fiddler's swag I wondered why he didn't want to work.

He was a metho drinker and when drunk would call out to teams of horses he could see beyond his fire.

"Whoa there! Hold up! Gee, Prince. Gee, Darkie. Come over. . . ."

Sometimes he ran round to the other side of the fire, swinging an imaginary whip with which he would flog some horse that angered him.

When he was sober he talked to me in a high-pitched voice.

"Don't stand there movin' from leg to leg like a hen in the rain," he said once. "Come over here."

When I went over to him he said, "Sit down," then added, "What's wrong with your leg?"

"I got Infantile Paralysis," I told him.

"Fancy that now!" he said, nodding his head sympathetically and clucking his tongue as he put more wood on his campfire. "Well, you've got a roof over your head, anyway." He looked up at me, "And a bloody good head it is; like a Romney Marsh lamb."

I liked these men because they never pitied me. They gave me confidence. In the world they travelled, being on crutches was not as bad as sleeping out in the rain or walking with your toes on the ground, or longing for a drink you had no money to buy. They saw nothing but the track ahead of them; they saw brighter things ahead of me.

Once, when I said to The Fiddler, "This is a good place to camp, isn't it?" he glanced round and said, "Yes, I suppose it is—to a bloke who hasn't got to camp here." He gave a scornful laugh. "A cocky said to me once, 'You blokes are never satisfied. If a bloke gives you cheese you'll want to fry it.'

" 'Yes,' I told him. 'That's me.'

"I've seen the time when I've been on the track and I've

thought if I only had tea and sugar I'd be right; then when I've got tea and sugar I want a smoke, and when I've got a smoke I want a good camp, and when I've got a good camp I want something to read. 'You don't happen to have any reading matter on you, do ya?' I asked this cocky. 'I can see I won't get any tucker out of you.'"

The Fiddler was the only swagman I met who carried a frying pan. He took it from his tucker bag and looked at it with satisfaction. Then he turned it over and looked at the bottom which he tapped with his finger.

"A solid pan, this . . ." he said. "I picked it up near Mildura."

He took some liver wrapped in newspaper from his tucker bag and frowned at it for a moment.

"Liver is the worst meat in the world to spoil your pan," he said, pursing his lips so that his black moustache jutted forward contemplatively. "It sticks like a plaster."

Like all swagmen, he was preoccupied with the weather. He was always studying the sky and speculating as to whether it was going to rain. He did not carry a tent in his swag, just the usual two blue blankets rolled round a few tattered garments and two or three tobacco tins containing his possessions.

"A hundred and sixty points of rain fell on me one night near Elmore," he told me. "It was too bloody dark to move and I sat there with me back to a post just thinkin'. Next morning there was mud everywhere and I had to plough through it. There won't be any rain tonight; it's too cold. She's comin' up, though. Might strike here tomorrow afternoon."

I told him he could sleep in the chaff house.

"What about your old man?" he asked.

"He's all right," I assured him. "He'll make you a mattress out of straw."

"That was him I was talking to this afternoon, was it?"

"Yes."

"He struck me as a good bloke. He rigs himself out flash but he talked to me just like I'm talkin' to you."

"Well, that's right, isn't it?"

"Course it's right. I think I will sleep in your chaff house," he added. "I been on a bender and I'm crook in the guts." He frowned at the pan in which the liver was sizzling. "I had terrible nightmares all night last night; dreamt I was on the track and the rain was comin' down hell for leather. Me billy had a hole in it and I couldn't make tea. Hell! I woke up sweatin'."

Another swagman came walking down the road while we were talking. He was a short, thick-set man with a beard and his swag was long and thin. His tucker bag hung loosely in front of him and he walked with a heavy, deliberate tread.

The Fiddler looked up sharply and watched him approach. I could see by his expression that he did not want this man to stop and I wondered why.

The newcomer walked over to the fire and dropped his swag at his feet.

"Goodday," he said.

"Goodday," said The Fiddler. "Where you makin'?"

"Adelaide."

"There's a long lead ahead of you."

"Yes. Got a smoke on you?"

"I'm on the butts. You can have a butt if you want it."

"That'll do." The man took the butt The Fiddler handed him, placed it delicately between his pursed lips and lit it with a glowing stick he took from the fire.

"Did you come through Turalla?" he asked The Fiddler.

"Yes. I lobbed here this afternoon."

"What's the butcher and baker like there?"

"The baker is all right, plenty of stale buns, but the butcher's no good. He wouldn't give you a burnt match. He'll shove you on the Douglas for a flap of mutton."

"Did you go to the back of the pub?"

"Yes. Got the butt of a roast there. The cook's all right—a big woman You could line off bricks with her nose. Ask her. Dodge her offsider. He's a little bloke; wants a drink for anything he gets you."

"Any Johns there?"

"No, but look out for the John at Balunga—that's further on —he's crook. He'll dwell on you if you go on the grog."

"I'm only holding a deener, so to hell with him!"

"You'll be all right further north," said The Fiddler. "I see they've had rain up there so every cocky'll be in at the pubs. You'll get a guts full there."

He cut a thick slice of bread from a loaf mother had given

him, divided the liver and placed one of the pieces on the bread which he handed to the man.

"Here, get that into you."

"Thanks," said the man. He munched at it for a while then asked, "You don't happen to have a needle and thread on you, do ya?"

"No," said The Fiddler.

The man looked at a split in the knee of his trousers. "A pin?"

"No."

"My boots are crook, too. What do they pay for harvesting round here?"

"Seven bob a day."

"That's right," said the man sourly. "Seven bob a day and they pay you off on Saturday so they won't have to feed you on Sunday. Have you got another butt on you?" he added.

"No, I'm hanging on to these," said The Fiddler. "There's a dance on at Turalla tonight. You'll get plenty of butts round the door in the morning. I reckon you'd better get movin' or she'll be dark before you strike Turalla."

"Yes," said the man slowly, "I suppose I'd better." He rose to his feet. "Straight on?" he asked swinging his swag on to his shoulder in one movement.

"Don't take the first turn, take the second. It's about two miles."

When he had gone I said to The Fiddler, "Wasn't that fellow any good?"

"He was humping a cigarette swag," explained The Fiddler. "We all dodge blokes with a swag like that. They never have anything. They bot on you for the lot. If that fellow joined up with you, you'd take all the skin off him draggin' him. Now show me where this chaff house is."

I took him up to the chaff house where father, having seen me talking to him, had already thrown in some armfuls of clean straw.

The Fiddler looked at it for a few moments in silence then he said, "You don't know how lucky you are."

"It's good to be lucky, isn't it?" I said, liking him a lot.

"Yes," he said.

I stood watching him unroll his swag.

"S'elp me!" he exclaimed looking around at me. "You hang

158

round like a drover's dog. Hadn't you better go in and have tea?"

"Yes," I said. "I'd better. Goodnight, Mr. Fiddler."

"Goodnight," he said gruffly.

A fortnight later he was burnt to death in his campfire eight miles from our place.

The man who told father about it said, "He'd been on the metho for a couple of days, they say. He rolled into the fire in the night—you know how it'd be. I was sayin' to Alec Simpson on my way down here, I said to him, 'It was his breath that caught fire, that's what it was.' He musta been fair full of metho. Once his breath caught fire the flame would go curling down through his guts like a fuse. By the living Harry, he'd burn! I was just sayin' it to Alec Simpson—Alec bought my chestnut mare, you know. I was just sayin' before I came down here that that's how he went all right and Alec said, 'By hell, I think you're right!'"

Father was silent a moment then said, "Well, that's the end of The Fiddler, poor beggar; he's dead and gone now."

23

Most men patronised me when they spoke to me, their usual attitude towards children. When other adults were listening it pleased them to be able to raise a laugh at my expense, not because they wished to hurt me but because my ingenuousness tempted them to play on it.

"Been riding any buckjumpers lately, Alan?" they would ask, a question I considered a serious one since I did not see myself as they did.

"No," I would say. "I will be soon, though."

This was considered by the one questioning me as worthy of a laugh and he would look towards his companions to include them in his mirth.

"Didya get that? He's going to ride buckjumpers next week."

Some men were abrupt and curt with me, regarding all children as uninteresting and incapable of being able to contribute anything of value to a conversation. Confronted with such men I could find no common level to communicate with them and I was silent and awkward in their company.

On the other hand I discovered that swagmen and bushmen, being lonely men, were often awkward and unsure of themselves when a child spoke to them but when they were met with an uncritical friendliness they were eager to continue the conversation.

One old bushman I knew was like that. His name was Peter McLeod and he was a teamster who carted posts from deep in the bush forty miles below our place. Each week he came out with his laden waggon, spent Sunday with his wife, then returned again, striding beside his team or standing upright in the empty waggon whistling some Scotch air.

When I called out, "Goodday, Mr. McLeod," he would stop and talk to me as if I were a man.

"Looks like rain," he'd say, and I'd say it did too.

"What's the bush like where you go, Mr. McLeod?" I asked him one day.

"As thick as the hairs on a dog," he answered, then added, as if the remark were a communication with himself, "Yes, she's thick all right. By hell, she's thick!"

He was a tall man with a shining black beard and legs that seemed longer than they should have been. His head bobbed when he walked and his big arms hung down a little in front of him. Father said he unfolded like a three-foot rule but father liked him and told me he was an honest man and could fight like a tiger cat.

"There's none round here could beat him at his best," he said. "He'd lock horns with anyone after a few beers. He's a tough, hard man with a soft heart but when he hits a man, the man stays hit."

Peter hadn't gone to church for twenty years. Father said, "then he went to vote against the Presbyterians joining up with the Methodists."

Once a Mission came to Turalla and Peter, after a week of heavy drinking, decided to become converted but he backed out like a frightened horse when he found they expected him to knock off drinking and smoking.

"I've been drinking and smoking to the Glory of God for forty years," he told father, "and I'll keep on for the Glory of God."

"That about sums up how he stands with God," father said. "I don't think he bothers much about Him when he's carting posts."

The bush Peter described to me seemed a magical place where kangaroos hopped quietly through the trees and possums chirred at night. It was the thought of an untouched bush that appealed to me. Peter called it "Maiden Bush"—bush that had never known an axe.

But it was so far away. It took Peter two and half days to reach the post-splitters' camp and he slept beside his waggon for a week.

"I wish I were you," I told him.

It was September and I was on holidays, the school being closed for a week. I had followed Peter's team in my chair, wanting to see his five horses drink from the trough. He carried a bucket to the two shafters and I sat in my chair and watched him.

"Why's that?" he asked.

"Then I could see the maiden bush," I told him.

"Hold up!" he sang out to the horse who was nosing the bucket he was lifting to her. She began drinking with a sucking noise.

"I'll take you there," he said, "I want a good bloke to help me. Yes, I'll take you any time you like."

"Will you?" I asked, unable to hide my excitement.

" 'Course I will," he said. "You ask your old man if you can come."

"When are you going?"

"I leave at five tomorrow morning from the house. You get down there at five and I'll take you."

"All right, Mr. McLeod," I said. "Thank you, Mr. McLeod. I'll be there at five."

I didn't want to discuss it further. I set off for home as fast as my arms would take me.

When I told father and mother that Mr. McLeod said he would take me to the bush, father looked surprised and mother asked, "Are you sure he meant it, Alan?"

"Yes, yes," I said quickly. "He wants me to help him. We're good mates. He said we were once. He told me to ask dad if I could go."

"What did he say to you?" asked father.

"He told me to be down at his place at five in the morning if you let me go."

Mother looked questioningly at father and he answered her glance.

"Yes, I know, but it'll all pay off in the end."

"It's not the trip so much," she said. "It's the drink and the bad language. You know what it's like when men are shut up in the bush."

"There'll be grog and bad language all right," father agreed. "Make no mistake about that. But that won't hurt him. It's the kid who never sees men grogging up who takes to it when he grows up. Swearing's the same—the kid who never hears bad language swears like a trooper when he's a man."

Mother looked at me and smiled. "So you're going to leave us, are you?" she said.

"Only a week," I said, feeling guilty. "I'll tell you all about it when I come home."

"Did Mr. McLeod mention anything about tucker?" she asked.

"No," I said.

"What have you got in the house?" Father looked at mother.

"I've got that round of corned beef for tonight's tea."

"Toss it into a bag with a couple of loaves of bread. That'll do him. Peter'll have tea."

"I've got to leave here at four," I said. "I mustn't be late."

"I'll wake you," mother promised.

"Help Peter as much as you can, son," said father. "Show him the breed holds good. Light his campfire for him while he feeds the horses. There's lots of jobs you can do."

"I'll work," I said. "My word, I will!"

Mother didn't have to wake me. I heard the creak of a board in the passage floor as she came out of her bedroom. I jumped out of bed and lit the candle. It was dark and cold and for some reason I felt depressed.

When I joined her she had lit the fire in the stove and was preparing my breakfast.

I hurried into Mary's room and woke her up. "Don't forget to feed the birds, will you, Mary?" I said. "Let Pat out for a fly about five. The possum's got plenty of green leaves but you'll have to give him bread. You'll have to change all the water today because I forgot, and the parrot loves thistles. There's one growing behind the stable."

"All right," she promised sleepily. "What time is it?"

"A quarter to four."

"Oo, dear!" she exclaimed.

Mother had scrambled me an egg and I began eating it with unnecessary haste.

"Don't gulp your food down like that, Alan," she said. "There is plenty of time. Did you wash yourself properly?"

"Yes."

"Behind the ears?"

"Yes, all round my neck."

"I've put some things in this little bag for you. Don't forget to clean your teeth with salt every morning. The brush is in the bag. And I've put in those old trousers of yours. Are your boots clean?"

"I think so."

She looked down at them. "No, they're not. Take them off and I'll black them."

She broke a piece off a stick of blacking and mixed it with water in a saucer. I stood fidgeting while she rubbed the black liquid over my boots, impatient to be gone. She brushed them till they shone and helped me put them on.

"I've taught you how to tie a bow," she said. "Why will you knot your laces?"

She carried the two sugar bags out to the buggy shed where I kept my chair and struck a match while I stacked them on the footboard and tied my crutches to the side.

The darkness had a bite of frost in it and I could hear a willy wagtail whistling from the old redgum. I had never been up so early before and I was excited with this new day that was still unspoilt by people, still silent with sleep.

"No one in the world is up yet, are they?" I said.

"No, you're the first up in the world," mother said. "Be a good boy, won't you?"

"Yes," I promised her.

She opened the gate and I passed through almost at top speed.

"Not so fast," she called after me in the dark.

Beneath the trees the darkness was like a wall and I slowed down. I could see the tops of the trees against the sky and I knew the shape of each of them. I knew where the holes in the road were and where it was better to cross the road and travel on the wrong side to avoid bad patches.

It was good to be alone and free to do as I wished. No grown-up was guiding me now. Everything I did was a direction from myself. I wanted it to be a long way to Peter McLeod's, but I wanted to get there quickly.

Once I had left the lane and passed on to the main road I could go faster and my arms were beginning to ache by the time I reached Peter's gate.

As I came down the track towards his house I could hear the iron shoes of the horses striking the cobblestoned floor of the stable. Though Peter and the horses were hidden in darkness I could see them with eyes created by sound. Tug chains clinked to impatient stamping, grains of chaff were snorted from nostrils and the stable door clattered as a horse bumped it passing out. Peter's voice yelled commands, a dog yelped and roosters began crowing from the fowlyard.

Peter was yoking up the horses when I pulled up in front of the stable. It was still dark and for a moment he did not recognise me. He dropped the trace chain he was holding and stepped over to the chair, peering down at me.

"It's you, Alan. Strike me! what are you do—— Cripes, you're not coming with me, are you?"

"You asked me," I replied uncertainly, suddenly afraid I had misunderstood him and he had not meant me to come.

" 'Course I asked you. I've been waiting here for you for hours."

"It's not five yet," I said.

"No, that's right," he muttered, suddenly thoughtful. "Your old man said you could come, did he?"

"Yes," I assured him. "So did mum. I've got my tucker. Here it is." I lifted the bag to show him.

He suddenly grinned at me through his beard. "I'll hop into that tonight," then changed his tone, "Come on. Shove your cart in the shed. We've got to be on the road at five." His face became serious again. "Are you sure your old man said you could come?"

"Yes," I insisted. "He wants me to go."

"All right." He turned to the horses. "Move over!" he cried as he placed one hand on a horse's rump and bent to pick up the trace chain with the other.

I put my chair in the shed and stood watching him, holding my two bags like a newchum-traveller about to board a boat.

The waggon was a heavy wood-waggon with broad iron tyres and brake blocks of redgum worked by a screw handle projecting from the rear. Its woodwork was bleached and cracked with sun and rain. There were no sides but at each of the four corners a heavy iron standard with a looped top was thrust into a socket in the bolster. It had a floor of heavy, loose planks that clattered loudly on bumpy roads. Some stays thrown on to the floor added to the noise. There were two pair of shafts, one for each shafter.

Peter raised a pair of these with a heave, hooked the back chain that crossed the shafter's saddle on to the "traveller" hook on the shaft then walked round to the other horse standing patiently beside its mate.

He yoked them noisily, yelling, "Hold up!" "Get over!" or "Whoa there!" each time a horse moved or refused to respond to his hand.

The three leaders stood side by side waiting for him to hitch their connecting reins and hook up their traces. They were not so heavy as the two shafters. They were Clydesdales while the two shafters had Shire blood in them.

After Peter had yoked the horses he threw the nosebags and some bags of chaff on to the waggon, glanced into his tucker box to see if he had forgotten anything, then turned to me and said, "That's the lot. Hop up! Here, I'll take your bags."

I swung over to the front of the waggon, and, holding on to the shafts with one hand, I threw my crutches up into the waggon with the other.

"Do you want a hand?" asked Peter, moving forward uncertainly.

"No thank you, Mr. McLeod. I'm right."

He walked to the leaders' heads and stood there waiting. I lifted myself with my hands till I got the knee of my good leg on the shaft then reached up and grasped the crupper of the shafter beside me. I pulled myself up till I was resting on his rump. It was warm and firm and divided by the shallow valley of his back into two powerful mounds of muscle.

"Rest your hand on a good horse and the strength of him goes through you," father had told me.

From the shafter's rump I swung over into the waggon and sat down on the tucker box.

"I'm right," I called to Peter.

He gathered the reins from where they were looped on the off shafter's hames and clambered up beside me.

"There's a hell of a lot of men can't get into a waggon as good as you," he said as he sat down.

166

He paused with the reins taut in his hands: "Would you like to sit on a butt of chaff?" he asked.

"No, I like here," I said.

"Gee, Prince!" he called. "Gee, Nugget!"

The team moved forward with a jingle of trace chains and a creak of harness. Behind them the waggon lurched and rumbled. There was a faint light in the eastern sky.

"I like to get away at piccaninny dawn," said Peter. "It gives you a good working day then." He yawned noisily then suddenly turned to me. "Now, you're not running out on your old man, are you? He said you could come?"

"Yes."

He looked gloomily at the road. "I can't make your old man out."

24

THE leaders walked with slackened trace chains, only tightening them when we came to a rise or a hill. I thought this was unfair to the shafters.

"The shafters are doing all the work," I complained to Peter.

"Once the waggon's moving, there's no weight in it," he explained. "This team could pull hell out by the roots if I ask 'em. Wait till we get the load of posts on, then you'll see them all pull."

Dawn had broken and there was a pink glow in the east. From every clump of trees the magpies were carolling. I felt there could be nothing in the world more lovely than this—sitting behind a team of horses in the early morning and listening to magpies.

From a distant paddock came the voice of a man shouting at a dog, "Go behind there!"

"That's Old Man O'Connor bringing in the cows," said Peter. "He's early this morning. Must be going out somewhere." He thought a moment. "He'll be going to Salisbury's clearing sale. Yes, that's it, and it'll be the Abbot buggy he's after." His voice expressed annoyance. "What does he want to be buying Abbot buggies for when he owes me ten quid for posts?"

He slapped the reins angrily against the shafter's rump. "Get on there!" After a while he said resignedly, "That's what you get for trusting a man; they go round driving Abbot buggies and I go round in a waggon."

We passed through the deserted streets of Balunga as the sun was rising and soon we were following a track winding between timber that gradually grew thicker till only the bush was around us and the fences had gone.

The dust from the horses' hooves rose into the air and settled softly on our hair and clothes. The wheels brushed against the leaning scrub as we passed and the waggon lurched as the wheels dropped into holes worn in the track.

I wanted Peter to tell me stories of his adventures. I looked upon him as a famous man. He was the hero of so many tales told where groups of men gathered to yarn. In hotel bars, so father said, some men would say, "You talk about fights! I saw Peter McLeod fight Long John Anderson behind the hall at Turalla." And everyone would listen to his tale of the fight that lasted two hours.

"Yes," the man would say, "they carried Long John away on a hurdle."

Peter had only been beaten once in his long career as a fist-fighter, and that was when he was so drunk he could hardly stand, and a farmer with a reputation for back-pedalling in a row had hopped into him to pay off an old grudge. His sudden, furious attack left Peter stretched out cold on the ground. When he came round the farmer had gone, but Peter was down at his cowyard before sunrise next morning, to the farmer's astonishment, and clutching the top rail with his two powerful hands he roared, with reddened face, "Are you as good a man now as you were last night? If you are, come out here."

The farmer stood transfixed, a bucket half full of milk hanging from his hand.

"I—er—I couldn't fight you now, Peter," he complained plaintively, gesturing with his hand to express complete surrender. "You're sober. You'd kill me when you're sober."

"You hopped into me last night," asserted Peter, a little non-plussed by this attitude. "Come and have a go at me now."

"But you were drunk last night," argued the farmer. "You could hardly stand up. I'd never fight you sober, Peter. I'd be mad."

"Well, I'll be damned!" exclaimed Peter, incapable of directing the situation. "Come out here, you cow."

"No, I won't fight you, Peter; not while you're sober. Call me anything you like."

"What the hell's the good of that if you won't fight?" Peter was exasperated.

"I see your point," said the farmer agreeably. "Calling names gets you nowhere. How're you feeling?"

"Sore as a boil," muttered Peter, looking round him as if for direction. He suddenly leaned wearily on the rail of the fence. "I'm crook as a mangy dog this morning."

"Wait till I get you a taste," said the farmer. "I've got some whisky in the house."

Father reckoned Peter went home leading a crook horse the farmer sold him, but mother said the horse was a good one.

I wanted Peter to tell me some of these stories so I said, "Father told me you could fight like a thrashin' machine, Mr. McLeod."

"Did he now!" he exclaimed, with a pleased expression on his face.

He sat thinking, then said, "Your old man thinks a lot of me. We've got a lot of time for each other. They tell me he was a great runner once. I was looking at him the other day. He stands like a Blackfellow." He changed his tone. "An' he said I could fight, did he?"

"Yes," I said, then added, "I wish I could fight."

"Aw, you'll be a good fighter some day. Your old man could scrap and you're like him. You can take punishment. If you want to be any good you've got to be able to take punishment. Look at the time I got into a push of the Stanleys. There's four of them and they can all go. I didn't know them but I heard of them. One of them—I think it was George—followed me round the back of the pub abusing me and when I talked fight he said, 'Remember, I'm one of the Stanleys,' and I said, 'I don't give a damn if you're the four of them. Put 'em up.'

"Well, we're no sooner into it than his three brothers come round, and I've got the four of them on my hands."

"Were they all fighting you?" I asked.

"Yes, the lot. I closed in and threw one, and as he was going down I slipped my knee up into his belly and took his wind. The other three kept me pretty honest for a while, but I kept getting in low down—that's the only way to fight with your fists. Get him underneath. Don't worry over the face. If you want to paint him, do it after the wind is out of him.

"I got me back to a wall and gave them a different hand each time. I didn't have much up my sleeve, but I got 'em all down then chucked it. The game wasn't paying. I was taking too much punishment. But I got the verdict. Cripes, yes!" he said, pleased with the memory. "It was a fight and a half."

We were passing through a large clearing in the bush. A decayed dog-leg fence, erected from trees felled along its line, encircled the paddock, in which saplings and scrub marked the return of the bush. A disused, grass-grown track led from some sliprails to a deserted bark hut where thin saplings swept their leaves against the walls.

Peter suddenly roused himself from his thoughts and said, with a new eagerness, "This is Jackson's place. In a minute I'll show you the stump where young Bob Jackson broke his neck. His horse bolted and threw him, then two months later Old Jackson wrapped a bullock chain round himself and walked into the dam. I'll show you the dam after. The stump's not far now. Just along here. . . . It's about twenty yards in from the fence. There was a lump came up on his chest as big as my head. He must have landed fair on the stump. Now, where is it?" He stood up on the waggon, looking intently into the paddock. "There it is. Whoa there! Whoa, blast ya."

The horses stopped.

"Over there on its side . . . See it? Near that dead wattle. . . . Hold up!" he yelled to one of the horses which had lowered its head to pluck the grass. "I must have another look at that stump. Come over and I'll show you."

We climbed over the fence and walked to a fire-blackened stump that lay with its blunted root-butts beside a grassed depression in the ground.

"They say this knob here caught him in the chest and he hit his head here." Peter pointed to two prominent root-spikes on the stump. "His horse . . . Now, where did it gallop from . . . It came around here," he waved his hand in a half-circle that embraced a stretch of the paddock. "Over there a bit. . . . Then it turned at that messmate—he reefed it round there, I reckon—and made past that clump of fern, then came along this stretch of grass flat out. It must have shied from the stump here."

He stepped four paces away from the stump and measured the distance with his eye for a moment. "That'd be about where he left its back. It'd shy out here," he waved an arm towards the fence, "and he'd tumble to the right." He paused a moment gazing steadily at the stump. "He never knew what hit him."

When we returned to the waggon, he told me that Old Jackson went queer after his son's death.

"It wasn't exactly cranky. He was just like he'd gone broke—sad all the time."

When we came to the dam Peter reined in the horses again and said, "Well, there it is. It's deep near the far bank. Of course it's silted up since then. He walked straight in and never came up. His old woman and the other boy cleared out after that. She felt it terrible. Now you wouldn't find a straw to clean your pipe with on the place. I brought in the cart and shifted her bits of furniture to Balunga. By hell, when she saw me she looked like the Relief of Mafeking. She filled up when I was leaving her. I told her Old Jackson was a white man if ever there was one. But my old woman reckons that makes it worse. I dunno. . . ."

He started the horses then said, "They say a bloke's brain system goes when he drowns himself. Maybe so . . . I dunno. . . . But Old Jackson wasn't like that. He was a good bloke. All he wanted was a mate to say, 'Give it another go,' and he was right. The trouble was I was getting the horses shod that day."

25

THAT night we camped in a deserted shingle-splitter's hut. Peter unharnessed the team then took a pair of hobbles and a horsebell from a bran bag he had been carrying on the waggon.

I lifted the bell from the ground. It was a heavy, five-pound bell with a deep musical note. I rang it, listening to the sound that I always associated with clear mornings in the bush, when every leaf was wet with dew and the magpies were singing. I dropped it a few inches to the ground and Peter, who had been rubbing some neatsfoot oil on the hobbles, exclaimed sharply, "Hell! Don't do that! You mustn't drop a bell. It ruins 'em. Here, show me." He held out his hand for the bell.

I picked it up and handed it to him.

"This is a Mongan bell, the best bell in Australia," he muttered, examining it carefully. "I gave a quid for it and I wouldn't take a fiver for it. You can hear it eight miles on a clear morning."

"Dad said the Condamine bell is the best."

"Yes, I know. He comes from Queensland. The Condamine sends a horse deaf. It's too high a note. You bell a horse regular with a Condamine, he goes deaf. There's only two bells—the Mennicke and the Mongan, and the Mongan's the best. That bell's made out of a pit saw. And not just any pit saw, either. They pick one with a good ring in it."

"What horse are you going to put it on?" I asked.

"Kate," he said. "She's the only bell horse I've got. The others can't ring it properly. She's got a long gait and shakes her head. She swings it when she walks. I bell her and I hobble Nugget. He's the boss and they all stop with him."

He stood erect. "I'm going to put the nosebags on them for an hour first. They only get roughage in the bush here."

"I'll light the fire in the hut, will I?" I asked.

"Yes. Start her up and put on the billy. I'll be with you in a minute."

When he came into the hut later I had the fire going and the billy boiling. He threw a handful of tea into the bubbling water and placed the billy on the stone hearth in front of the fireplace.

"Now, where's your corned beef?" he asked.

I had brought my sugar bags into the hut and I took the round of beef in its newspaper wrapping from one of them and handed it to him.

He unwrapped it, pressed it with one thick, dirt-blackened finger and commented, "It's prime beef, this—a piece of silverside."

He cut me a thick slice and placed it between two huge pieces of bread. "This'll stick to your ribs." He filled two tin pannikins with strong, black tea and handed me one. "I've never seen the woman yet who can make tea. You can always see the bottom of the cup when a woman makes it."

We sat before the fire eating our bread and meat. Between each mouthful Peter lifted his pannikin and took two noisy gulps of tea. "Ah!" he would say contentedly as he put the pannikin down again.

After he had finished the last pannikin of tea he tossed the dregs into the fire and said, "Now, how's this leg of yours at night? Do you have to tie it up or anything?"

"No," I said, surprised, "it's all right. It just lies there."

"Go on!" he exclaimed. "That's good. Does it hurt at all?"

"No," I said. "I don't know it's there."

"If you were my kid I'd take you up to Wang at Ballarat. He's a fair marvel, that fellow. He'd cure you."

I had heard of this Chinese herbalist. Most people round Turalla regarded him as the man to go to when all other doctors failed. Father always snorted when he heard his name mentioned. He called him a "weed merchant".

"Yes," Peter went on, "this Wang never asks you what's wrong with you. He just looks at you and tells you. I wouldn't've believed it, mind you, but Steve Ramsay told me all about

174

him—remember Ramsay, the bloke that couldn't hold nothing on his stomach but his two hands?"

"Yes," I said.

"Well, Wang cured him. Steve says to me, when I had the crook back, 'You go to Wang and don't tell him what's wrong with you. Just sit there and he'll hold your hand. He'll tell you things that'll stagger you,' and by cripes he did too. I took a week off and drove up and he looked at me like Steve said—I never told him nothin'—I was paying him—let him do the finding. I sits there and he sits there looking hard at me and holding me hand and he says, 'What are you wearing that bandage for?' Yes, that's what he says all right. 'I'm not wearing a bandage,' I says to him. 'You're wearing something round you,' he says. 'Well, I'm wearing a red flannel belt, if that's what you mean,' I says. 'You'll have to get rid of that,' he says. 'Have you ever had an accident?' 'No,' I tells him. 'Think again,' he says. 'Aw, well, about a year ago I was thrown out of a gig and the wheel ran over me,' I says, 'but I wasn't hurt.' 'Oh yes you were!' he reckons. 'That's your trouble. Your side is out of position.' 'Hell!' I says, 'is that what's bloody-well wrong with me,' then he gives me a packet of herbs for two quid and mum boils 'em up for me—terrible taste it was. I never got a pain after."

"But that's your stomach," I said. "I want my legs and back made better."

"It all comes from the stomach." Peter spoke with conviction. "You've got blown up or something—like a cow on lucerne—and there's something left there you gotta get rid of.

"Like that girl up country Wang cured. Everybody knows about that. She was so thin she couldn't throw a shadow but she ate like a horse. She had all the doctors licked then she went to Wang and he says, 'Don't eat nothing for two days then hold a plate of steak and onions under your nose and breathe it in.

"Well, she does this and a tapeworm crawls out her mouth and keeps crawling out. They tell me it was a hell of a length. It keeps coming out till it falls all tangled-up on her plate. She got as fat as mud after. It must have been in there for years eating everything she swallowed. Only for Wang she'd of been well dead.

175

"Aw no, doctors know nothing when it comes to these Chinese herbalist blokes."

I did not think there was any truth in what he said though his story frightened me.

"Father said anybody can be a Chinese herbalist," I argued. "He said all you want, to be a Chinese herbalist, is to look like a Chinaman."

"What!" exclaimed Peter indignantly. "He said that! He's mad! The man's mad!" Then he added in a less aggressive tone, "Mind you, you're the only bloke I'd say that to. But I tell you this: a bloke I know—educated, mind you; he can read anything—he told me that over in China where these blokes come from, they're learning for years. After they've finished learning they're examined by blokes well up in doctorin' an' that. These blokes examine them to find out whether they know enough to be Chinese herbalists. What they do—they take twelve of these blokes at a time—the blokes that are learning, see—they take these twelve blokes into a room with twelve round holes in the wall going through into another room. Then they go out—anywhere. . . . On the street, say . . . And they look for people with twelve terrible diseases. Like, they'd say, 'What's wrong with you?' 'Guts ache.' 'Right, in you come.' Then someone else—'Me liver's gone.' Good—in him, too. Then blokes—say, with backache like I had . . . 'Right, you'll do.'

"And they get twelve like that and they take 'em all into the other room and make 'em shove their hands through these holes in the wall. See how it's comin' out? The blokes wanting to be herbalists, they look at the twelve hands and they write down what each bloke's got on the other side and if they get one wrong, they're out."

He gave a scornful laugh. "An' your old man says anyone can be a Chinese herbalist! Still, we gotta lot of time for each other. He's got some funny ideas, but I don't hold it against him."

He rose to his feet and looked out the hut door. "I'll hobble Kate and let 'em out, then we'll turn in. She's going to be a pitch-black, dark night tonight."

He looked up at the stars. "The Milky Way's running north and south, anyway. It's gonna be fine. It's when she's east and west you get the rain. Well, I won't be long."

He went out to the horses and I could hear him yelling out to them in the dark. Then he was silent and the soft notes of the horsebell came to me as the horses moved out into the bush.

When he returned he said, "I haven't had Biddy down here before. She comes from Barclay Station. Horses reared in open country are always frightened, their first night in the bush. They hear the bark flapping. She was snorting a bit when I let her go. Aw, well, she'll be all right. Now, what about a bed for you?"

He looked carefully round the earth floor of the hut then walked over to a small hole beneath the wall. He studied it a moment then took the paper in which the corned beef had been wrapped and stuffed it into the hole with his fingers.

"Might be a snake hole," he muttered. "We'll hear that paper rattle if he comes out."

He laid two half-filled chaff bags on the floor and flattened them till they formed a mattress.

"There you are," he said, "that should do you. Lie down there and I'll chuck this rug over you."

I took off my boots and lay upon the bags with my head resting on my arm. I was tired and I thought it was a beautiful bed.

"How's it feel?" he asked.

"Good."

"The oats might come through and stick into you. It's good chaff that; came from Robinson's. He cuts it nice and fine. Well, I'll turn in."

He lay upon some bags he had prepared for himself, yawned noisily, and pulled a horserug over himself.

I lay awake listening to the sounds of the bush. It was so good to be there I didn't want to sleep. I lay beneath my rug gripped by an exciting awareness. Through the open door of the hut the smell of gum and wattle released by the night came moving across my bed. The wild cries of plovers going over, the call of a mopoke, the rustles and squeaks and the possum chirrs of warning—these created a presence in the darkness and I lay there tense with listening, awaiting a revelation.

Then, softly through the other sounds, came the notes of the horsebell and I sank back relaxed into the chaff mattress, seeing, as I fell asleep, the long, striding gait and swinging head of Kate ringing her Mongan bell.

177

26

THE bush through which we travelled became more stately, more aloof. As the trees increased in height so did our isolation from them become greater. They thrust their pure, limbless trunks two hundred feet above the earth before crowning themselves with leaves. No struggling scrub cluttered their feet; they stood on a brown carpet of their own shed bark. Beneath them was a strange expectant silence, unbroken by bird cries or the chatter of creeks.

Our tiny waggon with its tiny horses moved slowly beneath them, sometimes scraping some huge root-spur as we followed a turn in the track. The jingle of trace chains and the soft thud of hooves on the springy earth were small sounds that did not venture beyond the nearest tree. Even the creak of the waggon took on a plaintive note and Peter sat in silence.

In patches of friendlier bush where beech trees grew the track dipped into creeks where the clear, shallow water ran sparkling over stones as smooth as eggs.

In open spaces where the thin, wild grasses scarcely hid the earth, mobs of kangaroos stood watching us, raising twitching nostrils to get our scent before bounding slowly away.

"I've shot 'em," Peter declared, "but it's like shooting a horse; it gives you a crook feeling." He lit his pipe and added mildly, "I don't say as it's wrong, but a lotta things that ain't wrong ain't right either."

That night we camped on the bank of a creek. I slept beneath a bluegum and as I lay on my chaff bags I could see the stars beyond its branches. The air was moist, cool from the breath of tree ferns and moss and the horsebell sounded a clearer note. Sometimes it rang with sudden vigour when Kate clambered up a bank or slipped when descending to the creek to drink, but it was never silent.

"We'll reach the camp today," Peter told me in the morning. "I'm due there just before lunch. I want to load up this afternoon."

The post-splitters' camp lay on the side of a hill. It came into view as we rounded a spur—an open patch shorn from a fleece of trees.

Above the camp, from which a scarf of thin, blue smoke was rising, the hill lifted to a skyline of bunched tree-tops glittering in the sun.

The track skirted this hill and emerged on to the clearing around which the heads of slain trees were piled in confusion.

In the centre of the clearing were two tents with a campfire burning in front of them. Blackened billies hung from a tripod over the fire and four men were approaching it from where they had been working on a fallen tree lower down. A team of bullocks stood at rest beside a stack of split posts, while the bullock driver sat on his tucker box beside the waggon eating his lunch.

Peter had told me about the men who were camped here. He liked Ted Wilson, a man with stooped shoulders, a wispy, tobacco-stained moustache, and merry blue eyes embedded in wrinkles. Ted had put up a slab house about half a mile from the camp and he lived there with Mrs. Wilson and his three children.

Peter's opinion of Mrs. Wilson was divided. He considered her a good cook but complained she liked "howling about people who died".

179

"She doesn't like blood, either," he added.

It appeared that Mrs. Wilson, after being bitten by a mosquito one night had left a patch of blood "the size of a two-bob bit" on the pillow.

"The way she went on about it," reflected Peter, "you'd think a sheep had been killed in the room."

Ted Wilson worked with three other men who camped on the site. One of them, Stewart Prescott, a young man of twenty-two, had wavy hair and wore snub-nosed ox-blood boots when he went out. He had a huckaback waistcoat with round, red buttons like marbles, and he sang "Save My Mother's Picture from the Sale" in a nasally voice. He accompanied himself on the concertina and Peter regarded him as a great singer, but "a proper darn mug with horses".

People called Stewart Prescott "The Prince" because of his flash clothes, and he gradually became known as Prince Prescott.

He had once worked in the bush below our home and had often ridden past our gate on his way to a dance at Turalla. Father rode into Balunga with him one day and when father returned he told me, "I knew that fellow couldn't ride; every time he got off the horse he did his hair."

Prince was always talking about going to Queensland. "There's money to be made up there," he used to say. "They're opening up the land."

"That's right," father agreed with him. "Kidman's opening up as much as he can get. He'll open up six foot of it for you after you've worked for him for forty years. Write and ask him for a job."

Arthur Robins, the bullocky, came from Queensland. When Peter asked him why he left that State, he explained, "Me wife lives up there," an explanation that satisfied Peter. Peter asked him what Queensland was like and he replied, "It's a hell of a place but you can't help thinkin' you'd like to go back there."

He was a little man with stiff, wiry whiskers in the midst of which a large nose stood naked to the weather. It was an undefended nose, red and pitted, and father, who knew Arthur, once told me that it must have tossed in the towel before Arthur was ready.

180

Peter thought Arthur looked like a wombat. "Every time I see him I feel like hiding the spuds," he told me.

Arthur did not mind comments on his appearance but he resented any reflection on his bullocks. He once told the barman at the Turalla pub, in explaining why he had just been fighting a mate, "I stood him abusing me, but I wasn't going to stand him running down me bullocks."

He was an alert, quick man given to seeking relief with the remark, "It's a hard life." He said it when he rose to begin work after a lunch or as he left to go home when an evening's entertainment was over. It was not a complaint. It expressed some long weariness that made itself felt when he was faced with his work again.

When Peter reined in the team near the tents the men were already filling their pannikins with black tea they poured from the billies on the fire.

"How are ya, Ted?" Peter called as he climbed from the waggon. Without waiting for an answer, he continued, "Did ya hear I sold the chestnut mare?"

Ted Wilson walked to a log, carrying his pannikin of tea in one hand and a newspaper-wrapped lunch in the other.

"No, I hadn't heard."

"Barry bought her. I gave him a trial. That leg'll never come against her."

"I don't think so," commented Ted. "She was a good mare."

"I've never bred better. She'll take a drunk man home and keep to the right side of the road every time."

Arthur Robins, who had joined the group when we arrived, shrugged his shoulders and commented, "There he goes. As soon as he gets talkin' he breeds that mare over again."

Peter glanced at him agreeably. "How are ya, Arthur? Loaded up yet?"

"I'm a bloke who works, of course. I'm thinkin' of takin' on a horse team and givin' up work."

"You'll die in the yoke," retorted Peter mildly.

I had not got out of the waggon with Peter. I was looking for my pannikin and when I climbed down and walked towards the group each man looked at me with surprise.

Suddenly, for the first time, I felt my difference. That I should suddenly feel this way astonished me. I hesitated, momentarily confused. Then anger stirred in me and I swung towards them with quick, determined thrusts of my arms.

"Who's this you've got with ya?" asked Ted in surprise, rising to his feet and watching me with interest.

"That's Alan Marshall," Peter informed him. "He's a mate of mine. Come here, Alan. We'll bot some tucker off these blokes."

"Goodday, Alan," said Prince Prescott, feeling a sudden satisfaction at knowing me.

He turned to the others, eager to explain my crutches.

"He's the kid that got Infantile Paralysis. He was terrible crook. They say he'll never walk again."

Peter turned on him angrily. "What the hell are you talkin' about?" he demanded. "What's wrong with you?"

This outburst astonished Prince. The other men looked at Peter in surprise.

"What's wrong with what I said?" asked Prince, appealing to his mates.

Peter grunted. He took my pannikin and filled it with tea. "Nothing wrong," he said, "but don't say it again."

"So your leg's crook, is it?" asked Ted Wilson, breaking the tension. "You've gone in the fetlocks, is that it?" He was smiling at me and at his words all the men smiled.

"I tell you," declared Peter impressively, standing erect with my pannikin held in his hand, "if you could sole your boots with this kid's guts they'd last for ever."

I had felt lost and alone amongst these men, a feeling that even Ted Wilson's words had failed to dispel. I had regarded Prince's remark as silly. I was determined to walk again, but Peter's anger gave it an importance it did not deserve, while at the same time rousing in me the suspicion that all these men felt I would never walk again. I wished I were home; then Peter's final remark burst upon me, and I experienced so great a feeling of elation that the effect of what had been said before was swept away in an instant. He had lifted me to the level of these men, but more than that, he had ensured their respect for me. This was what I needed.

I felt so grateful to Peter I wanted to express it in some way. I stood as close to him as I could and when I cut slices from the mutton he had cooked the night before I gave him the best piece.

After lunch the men began loading posts on to Peter's waggon and I went over to talk to Arthur, the bullocky, who was
preparing to pull out.

His team of bullocks, sixteen of them, stood quietly chewing
their cuds, their eyes half-closed as if they were concentrating
on the working of their jaws.

The heavy yokes of river oak rested upon their necks with
the keyed ends of the bows projecting above them. From the
start-rings hanging from the centre of each yoke the lead chain
passed from pair to pair till it reached the ring at the end of
the waggon pole.

The two shafters were shorthorn stags with thick, powerful
necks and heads like bulls. Their horns were short but the
horns on the bullocks were long and pointed. The leaders were
two Herefords, tall, rangy animals with mild, tranquil eyes.

Arthur Robins was busy preparing to pull out of the clearing.
His huge waggon was laden with logs.

"Over ten ton there," he boasted.

He wore faded dungarees and heavy, hobnail-boots with
iron tips. His greasy felt hat had slits cut round the crown and
through these he had threaded a strip of greenhide.

He shouted to his dog to come from beneath the waggon.

"Any bullocky who lets his dog walk under the waggon
doesn't know his job. The bullocks don't like it. Go behind
there," he ordered as the dog slunk out. "It makes 'em kick,"
he explained to me as he pulled his trousers higher on to his
hips and tightened his belt. "Well, that's about the lot."

He looked round to see if he had forgotten anything then
picked up his six-foot handled whip from the ground. He
glanced at me to see if I were in the way. Some of the pleasure
I felt in watching him must have been reflected in my face, for
he lowered the butt of the whip to the ground and said, "You
like bullocks, do you?"

I told him I did and, seeing he was pleased with me, I asked
him their names. He pointed to each bullock with his whip
and gave its name with some comment on its value in the team.

"Buck and Scarlet are the polers, see? You want thick necks
on the polers. Those two can move a load on their own."

There was a bull in the team called Smokey and Arthur said
he was getting rid of him.

"If you yoke a bullock beside a bull, the bullock falls away fast," he said in confidential tones. "Some say the bull's breath is too strong, some say it is the smell of the bull, but the bullock always dies in the end."

He stepped closer to me, rested one of his legs by bending the knee, and tapped my chest with his fingers. "There's some cruel bullock drivers in the world," he said, his tone admitting me to some familiar world of his own. "That's why I'd sooner be a horse than a bullock." He raised himself and stretched his arm. "But I dunno; there's cruel teamsters too." He paused, thinking a moment, then added with some violence as if forcing the words from him, "An' you don't want to take no notice of what Prince said either. You gotta neck and shoulders on you like a working bullock. I've never seen a kid walk better."

He wheeled round with a shout and swung his huge whip.

"Buck! Scarlet!"

The polers moved into their yokes with slow, deliberate steps.

"Brindle! Poley!" His voice came back from the hills.

Down the long throat of each bullock in the team a moving lump of chewed grass passed smoothly as they swallowed their cuds in response to his voice. No bullock hurried. Each step they took to move into the yokes was a calculated one and not a reaction to fear.

When the lead chain was tight and each bullock lay leaning on its yoke with lowered head and taut hindquarters Arthur glanced quickly along the double line then shouted for the pull.

"Gee, Buck! Gee, Scarlet! Gee, Red!"

The sixteen bullocks moved as one. They pressed forward into the yokes with a slow power. For a moment of breathless strain the reluctant waggon with its load of posts remained motionless, then with a painful creaking it lurched forward and was under way rocking and complaining like a ship at sea.

Arthur strode beside his team with his dog at his heels, his whip over his shoulder. Where the track began to drop before a sharp descent he hurried behind the waggon, turning the handle of the screw-brake with urgent speed. As the steel tyres bit into the huge redgum brake blocks a painful shrieking came from the lumbering waggon. The sound sped round the hills, echoing from side to side, filling the valley with its anguish and startling a flock of black cockatoos into flight. They passed over my head with a powerful beat of wings and their mournful cries merged with the shrieking of the brakes in some sad protest that continued till the birds passed over the timbered crest and the waggon had reached the floor of the valley.

27

Tᴇᴅ Wɪʟꜱᴏɴ's house was half a mile off the main track. Peter always brought a case of beer down with him each trip, and it was the custom for the men to gather at Ted's house the night he loaded up, to drink and yarn and sing songs.

Arthur, the bullocky, always camped within walking distance on this night and two sleeper cutters, the "Ferguson Brothers", came over from their camp to have a drink and a yarn. Prince Prescott and the two other splitters were frequent visitors to the home, but on this night Prince brought his concertina and wore his huckaback waistcoat.

Ted rode on the waggon with Peter and me when we left the camp. When Peter called to me to climb aboard he turned to Ted and the three other splitters who were standing with him, and with his hand cupped to his mouth, said in a hoarse whisper, "Watch this now! You watch him. This kid's a marvel; won't let you help him. This is what I was telling you about," then dropping his hand, he addressed me in a voice intended to be casual, "Righto, Alan. Up you go."

Before he said this I had looked at the height of the load with some misgiving, but now that I had a reputation to live up to I approached the waggon with confidence. I clambered on to Kate's rump as I had before, but now the place I had to reach was high above me, and I knew I would have to stand upon her to reach a grip that would enable me to pull myself up. I grasped the end of one of the posts and dragged myself to a standing position with my good leg firm on her rump. From this height I swung myself to the top with little trouble.

"What did I tell you, eh?" Peter exclaimed, bending and thrusting a pleased face close to Ted's. "See it!" He straightened and flicked a scornful finger. "What's crutches to him—nothing!"

Peter and Ted sat with their legs hanging over the front of the load. The track to Ted's house was narrow and the branches of trees bent like bows as the bodies of the two men thrust them forward. As they passed, these branches sprang back and struck me sharply where I sat further back on the load. I lay on my back and watched them swish over me, delighting in the heavy rocking of the waggon and its laboured creaking. After a while the horses stopped and I knew we had arrived at Ted's home.

The house was built of upright slabs, the gaps between the slabs being packed with clay. A bark chimney filled one end and beside the chimney an iron tank was fed from a curled piece of bark that caught some of the rainwater shed by the bark roof.

There was neither fence nor garden to shield it from the encroaching bush. A thin, stringybark sapling bowed over it in the wind, and ferns grew thickly before the unused front door.

Near the back door an upright log formed a stand for a chipped enamel basin. The stains of soapy water streaked its sides and the ground around it was grey and muddy.

Four possum skins, stretched and nailed to the back wall with the flesh side out, glistened in the evening sun and from the lower branch of a wattle nearby a hessian meat safe swung gently to and fro.

The trunk of a tree fern formed a step for the back door and beside this a piece of hoop iron had been hammered into the tops of two pegs to form a scraper for removing mud from the boots of those about to enter.

Back from the house four sapling posts, supporting a bark roof, formed a shelter for a gig, the harness for which was hanging on the dashboard.

Peter pulled his team up in front of the shelter and I climbed down. Two children stood watching me as I turned and placed my crutches beneath my armpits.

One little boy, about three years old, was completely naked. Peter, looping the reins before tossing them on Kate's back, looked down at him with a pleased and interested smile on his face.

"Well!" he exclaimed. He reached out his rough, horny

hand and stroked the little boy's back with his fingers. "What a smooth little fella, eh! What a smooth little fella!"

The child looked solemnly at the ground, sucking his finger and submitting to Peter's caress with a suggestion of wariness in his stillness.

"He *is* a smooth little fella." Peter's fingers stroked his shoulders almost with wonder.

The other boy was about five. He was wearing long cotton stockings, but his garters had broken and the stockings hung round the tops of his boots like shackles. Braces made of rope supported his patched trousers, and his buttonless shirt only had one arm. His hair looked as if it had never been brushed. It stood straight out from his head like the hair on the back of a frightened dog.

Ted, who was unharnessing the horses, walked round from behind the leaders and, seeing his son, he stopped and looked at him critically, then shouted, "Pull up yer socks! Pull up yer socks! Peter'll think you're some new breed of fowl I've got."

The boy bent and pulled up his stockings while Ted watched him.

"Now take Alan here inside while we take out the horses. Tell mum we'll be in in a minute."

The woman who turned from the open fireplace to look at me as I entered wore an expression that suggested she was wagging a tail. Her face was fat and placating and she wiped her soft, damp hands hurriedly on a black apron patched with flour as she came over to me.

"Oh, you pore boy!" she exclaimed. "You're the cripple from Turalla, are you? Would you like to sit down now?"

She looked round the room, pressing her fingers against her full lips in a frowning moment of indecision. "This chair here. . . . Sit here. I'll get a cushion for your pore back."

She placed her hand on my arm to help me to the chair, lifting with such power that I had difficulty in keeping my armpit on the crutch. I staggered and, with a quick exclamation of concern, she seized my arm with both hands, looking towards the chair as if measuring the distance between me and salvation. I floundered to the chair, throwing my weight on the crutch she was not impeding while she held the other arm high in the air. I sank into the chair feeling confused and unhappy, wishing I were outside among men where my crutches seemed of little importance.

Mrs. Wilson stood back from the chair and viewed me with the satisfaction of a woman looking at a fowl she has just plucked.

"There, now!" she said happily. "Feel better now?"

I mumbled a "yes" of relief at being free of her grip and looked at the door through which I knew Peter and Ted would soon be entering.

Mrs. Wilson began questioning me on the "terrible disease" I had. She wanted to know did my leg hurt, my back ache, and did my mother rub me down with goanna oil.

"It's so penetrating it will go through a bottle," she informed me impressively.

She thought I might have a lot of acid in me and it might be as well for me to carry a potato in my pocket wherever I went.

"As it withers it sucks the acid out of ya," she explained.

She considered the possibility of my collapse while there and told me not to worry because Ted had the gig. Then she took a saucepan of boiled mutton that had been resting on two iron bars across the fire, sniffed it and complained about how hard it was to keep meat fresh in the bush.

I began to like her after she forgot I walked on crutches and talked of her own diseases. She busied herself round the kitchen as she talked, placing the steaming mutton on a large plate on the table and mashing the potatoes she had tipped from another saucepan. Straightening her back as if it hurt she told me in the confidential way of one imparting a secret that she would never make old bones.

I became interested and asked her why, and she replied darkly that her organs were all out of place. "I can't never have no more children," she informed me, then added, after a moment's thought, "Thank God!"

She sighed and looked abstractedly at the boy with the socks, who had been listening to us.

"Run and get Georgie's pants and shirt," she said suddenly. "They'll be dry now. I don't want him to catch his death of cold.".

In a moment the boy, whose name was Frank, brought them

in from where they had been hanging on a bush outside and she dressed Georgie, who had been looking solemnly at me while this was going on.

His mother gave a final pat to his shirt then stood back and warned him, "You come and tell me when you want to go anywhere next time. I'll smack you if you don't."

Georgie kept looking at me.

When Ted came in with Peter he slapped Mrs. Wilson so boisterously on the rump that I felt a sudden concern for her organs.

"How's the old woman?" he cried happily. He looked at the table to see what was for tea, then said to Peter, "This is a prime bit of mutton I got. I bought four ewes off Carter at half a crown a head. They were in good condition. Wait till you taste it."

28

WHEN the table was cleared after tea and the Miller lamp hanging by a chain from the ceiling was lit, Peter brought in the case of beer and he and Ted worked out on a piece of paper what each visitor was to pay for "the grog".

"We'll crack a bottle before the others come," Ted suggested after they had arrived at a figure, and Peter was agreeable.

Mrs. Wilson put the two boys to bed in the other room where I could hear a baby crying. After a while it stopped and she came out fastening her blouse. The two sleeper cutters had arrived and were sitting on a form beside the table. Their greeting showed they liked her.

"We certainly been punishin' those wedges today, Missus," one of them said to her, his big arms stretched out on the table as if they were too heavy for him to support.

"How're they splitting?" Ted asked him.

"Not bad. We're working on four-billeters. It's the quickest tree in the bush."

I wondered why a four-billeter was the quickest tree in the bush and had made up my mind to ask him, but Arthur Robins and the three post-splitters arrived and Ted began filling the pannikins lined up on the table.

Each man had brought his own pannikin and though the pannikins varied in size Ted poured the same quantity of beer into each of them.

After a few rounds Prince Prescott began playing his concertina. He swayed his shoulders in an exaggerated fashion, sometimes throwing his head back and flinging his arms above him where, for a moment, the concertina jigged in and out before being swept down again. Sometimes he hummed a few bars of a song as if testing his voice against the panting notes of the instrument.

"He's not warmed up yet," Arthur Robins told me in an undertone.

Arthur had sat beside me on a box near the fire. A gentle smile of anticipation never left his face. He was fond of songs with a kick in them, as he described it, and kept asking Prince to sing "The Wild Colonial Boy".

"What's wrong with the fella!" he exclaimed testily when Prince, absorbed in the "Valetta", failed to hear him.

"Give us 'The Wild Colonial Boy'," he demanded again in a louder voice. "To hell with that thing you're playing!"

The concertina stopped with a wheeze. "Righto," said Prince. "Here we go."

As he began to sing Arthur leant forward on his box, his lips moving to the words and his eyes bright with pleasure.

"There was a wild Colonial boy, Jack Doolan was his name,
Of poor but honest parents, he was born in Castlemaine;
He was his father's only hope, his mother's only joy,
The pride of both his parents was the wild Colonial boy."

This was father's favourite song and when there were men at our place and he had a few drinks in he would stand on the form and sing it, and when he came to the chorus he would shout, "Stand up when you sing this. Get on your feet, men," and when Prince broke into the chorus I took my crutches from against the wall and stood up, and I said with quick urgency to Arthur, "Stand up!"

"By God, I will, boy!" he said, and he rose to his feet and

crashed his tin pannikin on the table and he lifted his whiskery face and bellowed the chorus in a voice that should have come from a giant of a man. And I sang with him in high, unbroken tones and Peter and Ted and the sleeper cutters rose to their feet and sang too. We all stood up and the men crashed their pannikins on the table as Arthur had done and Mrs. Wilson clutched her hands on her breast and whispered "God love me!" in a tone of wonderment.

> "Come, all my hearties, we'll roam the mountains high,
> Together we will plunder, together we will die;
> We'll wander over valleys, and gallop over plains,
> And we'll scorn to live in slavery, bound down with iron chains."

"Ah, there's a song now!" said Arthur huskily as he sat down and held out his pannikin for more beer. "It puts great heart into a man when he can see no end to his labourin'."

The song had infected Peter with a desire to contribute something stirring to the gathering. He was too busy drinking to waste time singing a Scottish song, but he knew two lines of an Adam Lindsay Gordon poem that, throughout the evening, he repeated with an almost reverent respect.

They came to him now as he was standing filling a pannikin from a bottle and he suddenly stopped pouring and, holding the bottle and pannikin motionless in his hands, he gazed fixedly at the opposite wall and recited the lines in a deep, emotional voice.

> "Between sky and water, the Clown came and caught her,
> Our stirrups clashed loud as we lit."

For a moment after he finished he continued staring at the wall.

Arthur screwed up his face and looked at him speculatively. "He's still riding the Clown," he concluded, then turned his attention to his pannikin.

Whenever Peter recovered from the effect of his brief excursion into poetry he felt impelled to explain the quotation.

"You know what it means, don't ya? Some blokes miss it. This Clown is a fast jumper. He takes off well back, see, and he fairly flies over the waterjump. Now the other horse takes off first but the Clown, coming up fast, takes off behind him and catches him fair over the jump. That's what it means when it says 'between sky and water'.

"They land together. The other horse bores in as they land— you can bet that—and their stirrups clash. The Clown must have been a well-sprung horse, good bone with plenty of daylight under him. I'd like to meet the bloke that wrote it."

He swallowed a pannikin of beer and smacked his lips as he looked at the empty pannikin in his hand.

After a time it was hard to stop Prince singing. He sang "The Face on the Bar-room Floor", "The Luggage Van Ahead", and "What Will You Take for Me, Papa?"

Each song made tears run down the face of Mrs. Wilson. "Aren't they beautiful?" she sobbed. "Do you know any more?"

"Aw, yes, Mrs. Wilson, I know plenty more." Prince dropped his head modestly as he spoke. "I pick 'em up everywhere."

"Do you know 'The Fatal Wedding'?" she asked, leaning towards him hopefully.

"No, I don't know that one, Mrs. Wilson. I will, though. I'll get hold of it all right. I know 'Will the Angels Let Me Play?' Would you like to hear that?"

"Oo, yes!" said Mrs. Wilson. "It sounds lovely." She turned to Peter and Arthur who were arguing whether a team of bullocks could pull more than a team of horses.

"You two be quiet now," she demanded. "Prince is going to sing us a lovely song. You can argue after. Go on, Prince."

Peter dropped a hand with which he was emphasising a point and accepted the position. "All right. Into it, Prince." He leant back in his chair, his head nodding a little. "Let down the sliprails," he muttered.

Prince stood up and announced the title of the song: "Will the Angels Let Me Play?"

He bent over his concertina that began wailing beneath the curve of his body, then he straightened, flinging back his hair with a toss of his head, and began singing in a nasal voice:

"In a yard where children were playing games one day,
A little child on crutches was watching wistfully,
Tho' she tried so hard she couldn't play as other children do.
They said she was a bother and in their way too.
One night when all was silent, the Angels came that way
And took the little darling, whose sweet lips seemed to say:"

Prince swept into the refrain with a throb in his voice.

"Mother, when I go to heaven,
  Will the Angels let me play?
  Just because I am a cripple, will they say I'm in the way?
  Here, the children never want me, I'm a bother, they all say.
  When I go to heaven, mother, will the Angels let me play?"

As Prince sat down confident of praise to follow, Peter rose to his feet, staggered a little, then drew himself up and thumped the table, his glossy beard jutting out from his aggressive chin.

"That's the saddest darn song I've ever heard, but it should never have been sung in front of that kid here." He pointed a dramatic finger at me, shaking it in emphasis. "It's not the right song to sing in front of him." He turned and leant towards me. "Don't you take any notice of it, Alan." He sat down heavily and poured himself another beer. "Between sky and water the Clown came and caught her," he muttered.

I was astonished at his outburst. I had not connected the song with myself. I was touched by the plight of the little girl and kept wishing I were there to play with her. As Prince's voice kept on I saw myself thrashing every child who said she was a bother. I wondered why she didn't tell them off herself and concluded she must be a very little girl. But that I should consider myself like her was ridiculous.

Prince was annoyed with Peter. Just when he was preparing himself for praise Peter criticised him.

"What's wrong with it?" he protested to Arthur. "That song's all right. Alan knows he's crippled, don't he? So do we."

Arthur stood up and leant across the table so that he could speak confidentially to Prince.

"That's where you're wrong, Prince; he don't know he's crippled." He raised an emphatic finger to support each word with a gesture. "He'll never know it if he lives to be a hundred."

He drew himself up with lifted chin and firmly closed lips and looked at Prince sternly, anticipating disagreement from Prince, but Prince was suddenly humble, an attitude that changed the tone of Arthur's voice.

"I'm not saying it was a bad song," Arthur continued, "but why try and wake him up to what fools think?"

195

Prince admitted it would be better if I never woke up to fools.

"Oh, dear me!" exclaimed Mrs. Wilson, who was listening. "I've always said it's better not to know what's wrong with you. People with cancer an' that . . . Oh, it's terrible, terrible. . . ."

Arthur looked thoughtfully at her for a moment then shrugged and said to Prince, "Give us another song. What about something stirring like? Do you know that song about Ben Hall? There's a man now! Sing us that."

"I don't know the words of it, Arthur. How's it go?"

Arthur drew a deep breath and tucked his chin well down on his chest. "Only the robber rich men feared the coming of Ben Hall," he sang in a quavering, uncertain voice. He stopped and wiped the back of his hand across his mouth. "That's all I know, but, hell! it's a good song. You oughter learn it."

"I wish you'd sing 'There's Another Picture in my Mamma's Frame'," pleaded Mrs. Wilson.

"Strewth!" exclaimed Arthur contemptuously, and hurriedly swallowed a pannikin of beer.

"I heard a fellow sing that at a concert at Balunga one night," said one of the sleeper cutters. "It brought down the house. This bloke that sang it came up from Melbourne specially. I forget his name but they reckon he was a champion at singing. He used to get paid for it."

"I know two verses of it," Prince said. "Let's see if I can get the tune. I've sung it once but . . . Now, how's it go . . .?"

With his head on one side and his eyes closed he listened to the notes he squeezed from the concertina, then suddenly smiled and nodded. "She's right. I've got it."

"Quiet over there." And Mrs. Wilson looked at Peter and Ted who were talking together but not listening to each other.

"This saddle was a bit knocked about—the girth was no good—but I put it in the back of the cart . . ." Ted's voice suggested his remarks were confidential.

"I bought the grey for a fiver," Peter broke in, holding a pannikin of beer a few inches from his mouth while he gazed steadily across it at the wall. "I rode him twenty miles that night. . . ."

"It was a Queensland saddle," Ted interrupted, filling his pannikin.

"He never turned a hair . . ." said Peter.

"I bought a new girth . . ." Ted went on.

"Never raised a sweat . . ." Peter addressed the wall.

"Well, after that . . ." Ted was approaching the climax.

"Shut up, you two," said Arthur. "The missus here wants a song."

Peter and Ted looked at Arthur as if he were an intruding stranger.

"What . . ." began Ted.

"Prince is going to sing another song."

"Hop into it," Peter consented agreeably. He settled back in his chair and gazed at the ceiling. "We're listening."

Prince began singing:

> "Come, my baby, tell me why you're crying,
> Don't you see it pains your papa so?
> Every day for you nice things I'm buying,
> And I'd like to see you smile, you know,
> Then she said, I know you are the dearest
> And the sweetest papa of them all,
> If you love me truly, you will tell me surely
> Who's the lady's picture on the wall?"

Prince had the attention of all of us. Even Peter turned to look at him. He broke into the chorus with great confidence.

> "There's another picture in my mamma's frame,
> It's some other lady, her smile is not the same;
> My mamma was sweeter, I think it is a shame,
> There's another picture in my mamma's frame."

Mrs. Wilson wept quietly as Prince began the second verse.

> "Yes, my darling, it's a pretty lady,
> And she's going to be your new mamma,
> She'll be good and kind to you, and, maybe,
> You will love her, so 'twill please papa."

Arthur drank two pannikins of beer while Prince was singing, and when Prince was finished he informed me darkly, "Any man who marries twice wants his head read."

I was tired and I fell asleep in the chair while the singing continued. When Peter woke me up the party was over.

"Arise," he said in the tone of a Minister beginning a sermon. "Arise, and come with me."

We went out to the gig shelter where he had already prepared our beds. I snuggled into the chaff bags, but Peter stood holding on to one of the uprights and swaying. He suddenly raised his head and addressed the night.

> "Between sky and water, the Clown came and caught her.
> Our stirrups clashed loud as we lit."

29

FATHER wanted to know all that had happened to me on my trip with Peter. He questioned me closely about the men I met and asked me if I had talked to them.

When mother protested mildly against so many questions father quietened her with the rejoinder, "I want to know whether he can put his shoulder to a man."

He was pleased when I spoke excitedly about the staunchness of the horses and of how they pulled the laden waggon home with never a slackened trace.

"Ah! It's a good team," he commented. "Peter's got a great stamp of a horse in that Marlo breed. They're never off the bit." He paused, then asked, "Did he let you take the reins?"

He looked away when he asked me this, awaiting my answer with his hands suddenly still on the table.

"Yes," I told him.

He was pleased and nodded, smiling to himself. "A pair of hands is the thing . . ." he murmured, following a train of thought of his own. "A good pair of hands . . ."

He valued hands on a horse.

I remembered the feel of the horses' mouths on the taut reins. I remembered the power of the horses that came through the reins, the power they shared with me as they flattened in a heavy pull.

"The reins of straining horses takes all the strength out of you," father had told me once, but I had found it otherwise.

"You never want to worry over not being able to ride," he reminded me now. "I like a good driver, myself."

It was the first time for some years that he had mentioned my not being able to ride. After I returned from the hospital I talked about riding as if it were only a matter of weeks before

I would be in the saddle riding buckjumpers. It was a subject father did not like discussing. He was always silent and uncomfortable when I pleaded with him to lift me on a horse, but at last he must have felt compelled to explain his attitude for he told me that I could never ride—not until I was a man and could walk again.

He put his hand on my shoulder when he told me this, and he spoke earnestly as if it were important that I should understand him.

"When you ride," he said, "you grip the horse with your legs, see. When you rise to the trot you take your weight on the stirrups. It's not hard for a bloke with good legs. . . . He's got to have balance too, of course. He goes with the horse. But your legs can't grip, Alan. They're all right for getting you round but they're no good for riding. So chuck the idea. I wanted you to be able to ride, so did mum. But there you are. . . . There's often things a bloke wants to do but can't. I'd like to be like you but I can't, and you want to ride like me, and you can't. So both of us are crook on it."

I listened to him in silence. I did not believe what he said was true. I wondered that he believed it himself. He was always right; now for the first time he was wrong.

I had made up my mind to ride, and even as he spoke it pleased me to think how happy he would be when, one day, I galloped past our house on some arched-necked horse reefing at the bit as it fought my hold on the reins.

One of the boys at school rode an Arab pony called Starlight. Starlight was a white pony with a thin, sweeping tail and a quick, swinging walk. He had fine, sinewy fetlocks and trod the ground as if to spare the earth his weight.

Starlight became a symbol of perfection to me. Other boys rode ponies to school, but these ponies were not like Starlight. When the boys raced, as they often did, I watched Starlight stride to the lead, glorying in his superior speed, the eager spirit of him.

Bob Carlton, who owned him, was a thin boy with red hair. He liked talking to me about his pony since my attitude encouraged his boasting.

"I can leave all the other kids standing," he would say, and I would agree with him.

200

Each lunch time he rode Starlight down to the road-trough a quarter of a mile away to give him a drink. It was a task that took him away from the games in the school ground and he would have avoided it if he had not been trained never to neglect his horse.

One day I offered to do it for him, an offer he quickly accepted.

"Goodo," he said happily.

He always rode Starlight bareback down to the trough, but he saddled him for me and legged me on to his back with instructions to let him have his head and he would take me there and back even if I never touched the reins.

I had already concluded that Starlight would do this and had decided to cling to the pommel of the saddle with both hands and not bother about the reins.

When I was seated in the saddle Bob shortened the stirrups and I bent down and lifted my bad leg, thrusting the foot into the iron as far as the instep where it rested, taking the weight of the useless limb. I did the same for my good leg, but since it was not as badly paralysed I found I could put some pressure on it.

I gathered the reins in my hands then grasped the pommel of the saddle. I could not pull upon the reins or guide the pony, but I could feel the tug of his mouth upon my hands and this gave me an impression of control.

Starlight walked briskly through the gate then turned along the track towards the trough. I did not feel as secure as I had thought I would. My fingers began to ache from my grip on the pommel, but I could not relax and sit loosely in the saddle believing that, if I did, I would fall. I felt ashamed of myself, but I was angry too—angry with my body.

When we reached the trough, Starlight thrust his muzzle deep in the water. I looked down the steep incline of his neck dropping away from the pommel of the saddle and I drew back, placing one hand on his rump behind the saddle so that I could avoid looking down into the trough.

Starlight drank with a sucking sound, but in a minute he lifted his muzzle just above the surface, with water running from his mouth, and gazed with pricked ears across the paddock behind the trough.

Everything he did was impressed upon me with a sharp vividness. I was sitting on a pony with no one to direct me and this was how a pony drank when you were on its back alone with it; this was how it felt to be riding.

I looked down at the ground, at the scattered stones against which a crutch would strike, at the mud around the trough in which a crutch would slip. They presented no problem to me here. I need never consider them when on a pony's back.

Long grass that clutched my crutches, steep rises that took my breath, rough uneven ground—I thought of them now with a detached, untroubled mind, feeling elated that they no longer could bring a momentary despair upon me.

Starlight began to drink again. I leant forward, bending down and touching the lower part of his neck where I could feel the pulsing passage of the water he swallowed. His flesh was firm and he was strong and fleet and had a great heart. I suddenly loved him with a passion and a fierce hunger.

When he had finishing drinking he turned and I almost fell but now all fear of him had gone. I grasped the pommel and hung on while he walked back to the school. He walked beneath me without effort, without struggle, stepping on the ground as if his legs were my own.

Bob lifted me off.

"How did he go?" he asked.

"Good," I said. "I'll take him down again tomorrow."

30

Each day I took Starlight to water. I bridled and saddled him myself then led him round to Bob who legged me on and placed my crutches against the school wall.

In a few weeks I could ride him without concentrating on keeping my seat in the saddle. I could relax and did not retain so intense a grip on the pommel.

But I still had no control over the reins. I could not rein the pony in or direct him. When walking in the bush or riding in my chair I pondered over this problem. Before dropping off to sleep at night I designed saddles with sliding grips on them, with backs like chairs, with straps to bind my legs to the horse, but when on Starlight's back I realised these saddles would not help me. I had to learn to balance myself without the aid of my legs, to ride without holding on.

I began urging Starlight into a jog trot the last few yards to the trough, and gradually increased this distance till I was jogging over the last hundred yards.

It was not a pleasant gait. I bumped violently up and down on the saddle, unable to control my bouncing body by taking some of the shock with my legs.

The children watched me but were not critical of my riding. I had my own way of doing things and they accepted it. My seat in the saddle was precarious and suggested I would easily fall, but after observing this and noting that I showed no fear of falling they lost interest.

Those who rode to school often set off for home at a gallop. It surprised me that they seemed to ride so easily. I became impatient to improve. Surely what they could do, I could do too.

But my mind kept demanding results that my body was incapable of producing. Month after month I rode to the trough but my riding was not improving. I still had to hold on; I had never cantered; I could not guide the pony. For a year I had to be satisfied with walking and jog trotting to the trough, then I made up my mind to canter even if I did fall off.

I asked Bob was it easy to sit a canter.

"Cripes, yes!" he said, "it's like sitting on a rocking horse. It's easier than trotting. You never leave the saddle when Starlight's cantering. He don't stride like a pony; he strides like a horse."

"Will he break into a canter without trotting fast first?" I asked.

Bob assured me he would. "Lean forward and lift him into it," he instructed me. "Clap him with your heels and he'll break into a canter straight off."

I tried that day. There was a slight rise approaching the trough and when I reached it I leant forward quickly and touched him with the heel of my good foot. He broke into an easy canter and I found myself swinging along in curves of motion, with a new wind upon my face and an urge to shout within me. Starlight jogged to a stop at the trough and when he began drinking and I relaxed I found myself trembling.

After that I cantered each day until I felt secure, even when he turned sharply at the school gates.

But I was still clinging to the pommel of the saddle.

Two tracks converged at the trough. One led past the school but the other turned up a lane behind the school and joined the main road on the other side of the building. This lane was rarely used. Three winding depressions made by the horses and waggons that were sometimes driven along it, wound through the grass between the enclosing fences.

One of these fences consisted of four strands of barbed wire stapled to the outside of each post. Following this fence was a pad made by the road cattle moving down to the trough to drink. Tufts of red hair clung to many of the barbs along the fence where the cattle had scraped their sides on the wire as they passed.

I had sometimes considered riding along this lane back to

the school but since I had no means of guiding Starlight, I had to go along the track he favoured.

One winter day I touched him sharply with my heel as he turned from the trough and he broke into a swift canter, but instead of following the usual track to the school he turned up the lane.

I was pleased. I had rested in this lane many a time when walking back from the foot of Mt. Turalla and I associated it with fatigue. Its tangly grass and ridgy tracks were not easy to walk upon, and now I looked down at them streaking swiftly beneath me, marvelling at the ease with which I passed above them. The troubling associations they always held for me did not now impress themselves upon my mind, and I looked at the rough earth with affection.

Starlight turned from the centre track and cantered along the cattle pad, a manoeuvre I had not anticipated. As he swung on to the pad I realised my danger and strained at the pommel of the saddle with my hands as if, in this way, I could turn him away from the fence with its waiting barbs.

But he kept on, and I looked down at my bad leg dangling helplessly in the stirrup and at the strands of barbed wire streaking past it a few inches away.

I was wearing long cotton stockings held up by garters above my knees. By bad leg was bandaged beneath the stocking that covered it, protection for the broken chilblains that, throughout the winter, never left me.

I looked ahead to where the pad moved closer to the posts and I knew that in a moment my leg would be tearing along the barbs. I was not afraid, but I felt resentful that I had to resign myself to this without being able to fight back.

For a moment I considered throwing myself off. I drew a breath and thought "now", but I could not bring myself to do it. I saw myself with a broken arm, unable to walk on my crutches. I looked back at the fence.

When the first barbs struck the side of my leg they dragged it back towards the pony's flank then dropped it as the pad curved away again. It fell back loosely, dangling free of the stirrup for a space before being snatched up and torn again. The barbs ripped through the stocking and the bandage and I felt the flow of blood on my leg.

My mind became still and quiet. I did not look at my leg again. I looked ahead to where the pad finally drew away from the fence at the end of the lane and resigned myself to a torn leg and to pain.

It seemed a long way to the end of the lane, and Starlight reached it without a falter in his swinging canter. He turned at the corner and came back to the school with eager head and pricked ears, but I was limp upon him.

Bob and Joe helped me off.

"Strewth! What's wrong?" asked Joe, bending and looking anxiously at my face.

"He went up the lane and dragged my leg against the barbed wire," I told him.

"What did he do that for?" asked Bob incredulously, stooping to look at my leg. "He never does that. Hell, your leg's bleeding. It's all cut. Your sock's all torn. What did he go up there for? You'll have to see a doctor or something. Cripes, your leg's crook!"

"Fix it up down the back before anyone see you," advised Joe quickly.

Joe understood me.

"I wonder who's got a handkerchief?" I asked Joe. "I'll have to tie it up. What kid's got a handkerchief?"

"I'll ask Perce," offered Bob. "Perce'll have one."

Perce was the siss of the school and was known to carry a handkerchief. Bob went to look for him and Joe and I went down to the back of the school, where I sat down and pulled my tattered stocking down round my ankle. I unwrapped the torn bandage and exposed the jagged cuts. They were not deep but there were several of them and they bled freely, the blood flowing sluggishly over the broken chilblains and the cold, bluish skin.

Joe and I looked at it in silence.

"Anyway, that leg was never any good to you," Joe said at last, anxious to comfort me.

"Blast it!" I muttered savagely. "Blast my leg. See if Bob's coming."

Bob came down with a handkerchief he had taken almost by force from Perce, who had followed him up to learn what was to happen to it.

"You've got to bring it back tomorrow," he warned me, his voice trailing off as he saw my leg. "Oo, look!" he exclaimed.

With the aid of the handkerchief and the torn bandage I already had, I bound my leg firmly, then rose on my crutches while the three boys stood back and awaited my verdict.

"She'll do," I said, after waiting a moment to see if its stinging would cease.

"She'll never bleed through all that rag," Joe pronounced. "No one will know."

31

MOTHER never knew I had torn my leg. I always attended to my chilblains myself after she had given me a dish of hot water, a clean bandage and wadding to put between my toes. Sometimes I thought I would have to tell her as the cuts refused to heal on the cold flesh, but when the warm weather came they healed.

I continued taking Starlight to the trough but now I never cantered him till he was on the track to the school and the turn-off to the lane was behind him.

I had often tried to ride with only one hand clinging to the pommel of the saddle, but the curvature of my spine made me lean to the left and one hand on the pommel did not prevent a tendency for me to fall in that direction.

One day, while Starlight was walking, I began gripping the saddle in various places, searching for a more secure position on which to hold. My left hand, owing to my lean in that direction, could reach far lower than my right while I was still relaxed. I moved my seat a little to the right in the saddle then thrust my left hand under the saddle flap beneath my leg. Here I could grasp the surcingle just where it entered the flap after crossing the saddle. I could bear down upon the inner saddle pad to counter a sway to the right or pull on the surcingle to counter a sway to the left.

For the first time I felt completely safe. I crossed the reins, gripping them with my right hand, clutched the surcingle and urged Starlight into a canter. His swinging stride never moved me in the saddle. I sat relaxed and balanced, rising and falling with the movement of his body and experiencing a feeling of security and confidence I had not known before.

Now I could guide him. With a twist of my hand I could turn him to the right or the left and as he turned I could lean with him and swing back again as he straightened to an even stride. My grip on the surcingle braced me to the saddle, a brace that could immediately adjust itself to a demand for a steadying push or pull.

I cantered Starlight for a little while then, on a sudden impulse, I yelled him into greater speed. I felt his body flatten as he moved from a canter into a gallop. The undulating swing gave way to a smooth run and the quick tattoo of his pounding hooves came up to me like music.

It was too magnificent an experience to repeat, to waste in a day. I walked him back to the school humming a song. I did not wait for Bob to leg me off; I slid off on my own and fell over on the ground. I crawled to my crutches against the wall then stood up and led Starlight to the pony yard. When I unsaddled him and let him go I stood leaning on the fence just watching him till the bell rang.

I did not concentrate on my lessons that afternoon. I kept thinking about father and how pleased he would be when I could prove to him I could ride. I wanted to ride Starlight down next day and show him, but I knew the questions he would ask me, and I felt that I could not truthfully say I could ride until I could mount and dismount without help.

I would soon learn to get off, I reflected. If I got off beside my crutches I could cling to the saddle with one hand till I got hold of them and put them beneath my arms. But getting on was another matter. Strong legs were needed to rise from the ground with one foot in the stirrup. I would have to think of another way.

Sometimes when romping at home I would place one hand on top of our gate and one on the armpit rest of a crutch, then raise myself slowly till I was high above the gate. It was a feat of strength I often practised, and I decided to try it with Starlight in place of the gate. If he stood I could do it.

I tried it next day but Starlight kept moving and I fell several times. I got Joe to hold him, then placed one hand on the pommel and the other on the top of the two crutches standing together. I drew a breath, then swung myself up and on to the saddle with one heave. I slung the crutches on my right arm, deciding to carry them but they frighten Starlight and I had to hand them to Joe.

Each day Joe held Starlight while I mounted but in a fortnight the pony became so used to me swinging on to the saddle in this fashion that he made no attempt to move till I was seated. I never asked Joe to hold him after that, but I still could not carry my crutches.

I showed Bob how I wanted to carry them, slung on my right arm, and asked him would he ride Starlight round while he carried my crutches in this fashion. He did it each afternoon after school was out and Starlight lost his fear of them. After that he let me carry them.

When cantering they clacked against his side and at a gallop they swung out, pointing backwards, but he was never afraid of them again.

Starlight was not tough in the mouth and I could easily control him with one hand on the reins. I rode with a short rein so that, by leaning back, I added the weight of my body to the strength of my arm. He responded to a twist of the hand when I wished him to turn and I soon began wheeling him like a stockpony. By thrusting against the saddle pad with the hand that held the surcingle I found I could rise to the trot, and my bumping days were over.

Starlight never shied. He kept a straight course and because of this I felt secure and was not afraid of being thrown. I did not realise that normal legs were needed to sit a sudden shy since I had never experienced one. I was confident that only a bucking horse could throw me and I began riding more recklessly than the boys at school.

I galloped over rough ground, meeting the challenge it presented to my crutches by spurning it with legs as strong as steel—Starlight's legs which now I felt were my own.

Where other boys avoided a mound or bank on their ponies, I went over them, yet when walking it was I who turned away and they who climbed them.

Now their experiences could be mine and I spent the school dinner hour in seeking out places in which I would have found difficulty in walking, so that in riding through or over them, I became the equal of my mates.

Yet I did not know that such was my reason. I rode in these places because it pleased me. That was my explanation.

Sometimes I galloped Starlight up the lane. The corner at the end was sharp and turned on to a metal road. The Presbyterian Church was built on the opposite corner and it was known as the "Church Corner".

One day I came round this corner at a hand gallop. It was beginning to rain and I wanted to reach the school before I got wet. A woman walking along the pathway in front of the church suddenly put up her umbrella and Starlight swerved away from it in a sudden bound.

I felt myself falling and I tried to will my bad leg to pull the foot from the stirrup. I had a horror of being dragged. Father had seen a man dragged with his foot caught in the stirrup and I could never forget his description of the galloping horse and the bouncing body.

When I hit the metal and knew I was free of the saddle I only felt relief. I lay there a moment wondering whether any bones were broken then sat up and felt my legs and arms which were painful from bruises. A lump was rising on my head and I had a gravel rash on my elbow.

Starlight had galloped back to the school and I knew that Bob and Joe would soon be along with my crutches. I sat there dusting my trousers when I noticed the woman who had opened the umbrella. She was running towards me with such an expression of alarm and concern upon her face that I looked quickly round to see if something terrible had occurred behind me, something of which I was not aware. But I was alone.

"Oh!" she cried. "Oh! You fell! I saw you. You poor boy! Are you hurt? Oh, I'll never forget it!"

I recognised her as Mrs. Conlon whom mother knew and I thought, "She'll tell mum I fell. I'll have to show dad I can ride tomorrow."

Mrs. Conlon hurriedly placed her parcels on the ground and put her hand on my shoulder, peering at me with her mouth slightly open.

"Are you hurt, Alan? Tell me. What will your poor mother say? Say something."

"I'm all right, Mrs. Conlon," I assured her. "I'm waiting for my crutches. Joe Carmichael will bring my crutches when he sees the pony."

I had faith in Joe attending to things like that. Bob would come running down full of excitement, announcing an accident to the world; Joe would be running silently with my crutches, his mind busy on how to keep it quiet.

"You should never ride ponies, Alan," Mrs. Conlon went on while she dusted my shoulders. "It'll be the death of you, see if it isn't." Her voice took on a tender, kindly note and she knelt beside me and bent her head till her face was close to mine. She smiled gently at me. "You're different from other boys. You never want to forget that. You can't do what they do. If your poor father and mother knew you were riding ponies it would break their hearts. Promise me you won't ride again. Come on, now."

I saw with wonder that there were tears in her eyes and I wanted to comfort her, to tell her I was sorry for her. I wanted to give her a present, something that would make her smile and bring her happines. I saw so much of this sadness in grown-ups who talked to me. No matter what I said I could not share my happiness with them. They clung to their sorrow. I could never see a reason for it.

Bob and Joe came running up and Joe was carrying my crutches. Mrs. Conlon sighed and rose to her feet, looking at me with tragic eyes as Joe helped me up and thrust my crutches beneath my arms.

"What happened?" he demanded anxiously.

"He shied and tossed me," I said. "I'm all right."

"Now we'll all shut up about this," whispered Joe looking sideways at Mrs. Conlon. "Keep it under your hat or they'll never let you on a horse again."

I said goodbye to Mrs. Conlon who reminded me, "Don't forget what I told you, Alan," before she went away.

"There's one thing," said Joe, looking me up and down as we set off for the school. "There's no damage done; you're walking just as good as ever."

32

NEXT day I rode Starlight home during lunch hour. I did not hurry. I wanted to enjoy my picture of father seeing me ride. I thought it might worry mother but father would place his hand on my shoulder and look at me and say, "I knew you could do it," or something like that.

He was bending over a saddle lying on the ground near the chaff house door when I rode up to the gate. He did not see me. I stopped at the gate and watched him for a moment then called out, "Hi!"

He did not straighten himself but turned his head and looked back towards the gate behind him. For a moment he held this position while I looked, smiling, at him, then he quietly stood erect and gazed at me for a moment.

"You, Alan!" he said, his tone restrained as if I were riding a horse a voice could frighten into bolting.

"Yes," I called. "Come and see me. You watch. Remember when you said I'd never ride? Now, you watch. Yahoo!" I gave the yell he sometimes gave when on a spirited horse and leant forward in the saddle with a quick lift and a sharp clap of my good heel on Starlight's side.

The white pony sprang forward with short, eager bounds, gathering himself until, balanced, he flattened into a run. I could see his knee below his shoulder flash out and back like a piston, feel the drive of him and the reach of his shoulders to every stride.

I followed our fence to the wattle clump then reefed him back and round, leaning with him as he propped and turned in a panel's length. Stones scattered as he finished the turn; his head rose and fell as he doubled himself to regain speed: then

I was racing back again while father ran desperately towards the gate.

I passed him, my hand on the reins moving forward and back to the pull of Starlight's extended head. Round again and back to a skidding halt with Starlight's chest against the gate. He drew back dancing, tossing his head, his ribs pumping. The sound of his breath through his distended nostrils, the creak of the saddle, the jingle of the bit were the sounds I had longed to hear while sitting on the back of a prancing horse and now I was hearing them and smelling the sweat from a completed gallop.

I looked down at father, noticing with sudden concern that he was pale. Mother had come out of the house and was hurrying towards us.

"What's wrong, dad?" I asked, quickly.

"Nothing," he said. He kept looking at the ground and I could hear him breathing.

"You shouldn't have run like that to the gate," I said. "You winded yourself."

He looked at me and smiled, then turned to mother who reached out her hand to him as she came up to the gate.

"I saw it," she said.

They looked into each other's eyes a moment.

"He's you all over again," mother said, then turning to me, "You learned to ride yourself, Alan, did you?"

"Yes," I said, leaning on Starlight's neck so that my head was closer to theirs. "For years I've been learning. I've only had one buster; that was yesterday. Did you see me turn, dad?" I turned to father. "Did you see me bring him round like a stockhorse? What do you think? Do you reckon I can ride?"

"Yes," he said. "You're good; you've got good hands and you sit him well. How do you hold on? Show me."

I explained my grip on the surcingle, told him how I used to take Starlight to drink and how I could mount or dismount with the aid of my crutches.

"I've left my crutches at school or I'd show you," I said.

"It's all right . . . Another day . . . You feel safe on his back?"

"Safe as a bank."

"Your back doesn't hurt you, does it, Alan?" mother asked.

"No, not a bit," I said.

"You'll always be very careful, won't you, Alan? I like seeing you riding but I wouldn't like to see you fall."

"I'll be very careful," I promised, then added, "I must go back to school; I'll be late."

"Listen, son," father said, looking up at me with a serious face. "We know you can ride now. You went past that gate like a bat out of hell. But you don't want to ride like that. If you do people will think you're a mug rider. They'll think you don't understand a horse. A good rider hasn't got to be rip-snorting about like a pup off the chain just to show he can ride. A good rider don't have to prove nothing. He studies his mount. You do that. Take it quietly. You can ride—all right, but don't be a show-off with it. A gallop's all right on a straight track but the way you're riding, you'll tear the guts out of a horse in no time. A horse is like a man; he's at his best when he gets a fair deal. Now, walk Starlight back to school and give him a rub down before you let him go."

He paused, thinking for a moment, then added, "You're a good bloke, Alan. I like you and I reckon you're a good rider."

33

CARS were appearing on the roads. Behind streamers of dust they sped along highways designed for the iron-shod wheels of buggies. They wore corrugations in the metal, sent stinging pellets of gravel clattering against the dashboards of gigs they passed and honked their way through groups of road cattle, scattering them in fear. They had great brass lamps lit by acetylene gas, brass radiators and upright, dignified windscreens behind which men in dustcoats and goggles leant forward peering and clutching wheels they sometimes tugged at like reins.

Startled horses wheeled and plunged from the fumes and noise of their passing and angry drivers stood erect in buggies brought to a halt far out on the areas of grass that skirted the roadways, and cursed violently as they watched the receding dust.

Farmers left their paddock gates open so that frightened horses, fighting the reins, could be guided through into areas away from the road where they were held trembling and prancing till the cars had passed.

Peter Finlay was no longer a groom for Mrs. Carruthers; he was her chauffeur and wore a peaked cap and a uniform and stood with his heels together when he opened the door to let her out.

"What do you hug the road for?" father demanded of him one day. "Do you own the road? Everybody's got to get off on the grass when you come along."

"You can't run a car off the road like a horse," Peter explained to him. "I've got to stay on the metal and there's only room for one."

"Yes, and Mrs. Carruthers is the one," said father angrily. "It's getting so I'm frightened to take a young horse out on the roads. If I could get a horse that would face that car I'd drive straight at you."

After that Peter always stopped when father wanted to pass him with a young horse, but even then the horse went careering out on to the grass with father reefing on the reins and swearing.

He hated cars, but he told me they were here to stay.

"When you are as old as me, Alan," he said, "you'll have to go to the zoo to see a horse. The day of the horse is done."

He was getting fewer horses to break in and prices were rising, yet he managed to save ten pounds for some jars of brown ointment which mother rubbed into my legs. It was an American treatment known as the Viavi System and the salesman who sold it to father guaranteed it would make me walk.

Month after month mother massaged my legs, using jar after jar of ointment till none was left.

Father had no faith in it from the beginning, "but like a fool I hoped for a miracle," he commented bitterly when mother told him the treatment was over.

He had prepared me for its failure and I was not disappointed.

"I'm not going to waste any more time on cures," I told him. "It holds me back."

"That's what I think," he replied.

I was now riding ponies he had quietened and was having frequent falls. Ponies, newly-broken, shied readily and I could never learn to sit a shier.

I was convinced that each fall I had would be my last, but father thought differently.

"We all say that, son. We say it after every fall. When a bloke has his last tumble he don't know it."

But my falls troubled him. He was restless with indecision then, with sudden resolve, he began teaching me how to fall—relaxed and limp so that the blow from the ground was cushioned on yielding muscle.

"You can always beat a thing," he impressed upon me. "If not one way, then another."

He was quick with solutions to the problems presented by my crutches, but what I was to do when I left school—this he could not answer.

It was only two months to the end of the year and my final day at school. Mr. Simmons, the storekeeper at Turalla, had promised to give me five shillings a week to keep his books after I left school, but though it pleased me to think I would be earning money, I wanted work that would test me; that would demand the exercise of that part of my mind that was my possession alone.

"What do you want to be?" father asked me.

"I want to write books."

"Well, that's all right," he said. "You can do that, but how are you going to earn your living?"

"Men make money writing books," I argued.

"Yes, but only after years and years—and then you have to be well educated. Peter Finlay tells me writing a book is the hardest thing in the world—he's tried it. Mind you, I'm all for you writing a book; don't think I'm not, but you've got to learn first."

He stood in silence thinking for a moment and when he spoke again it was as if he knew I was going to be a writer some day.

"When you write," he said, "be like Robert Blatchford. That's the bloke that wrote Not Guilty and it's a great book. It was written to help people.

"You see," he went on, "it's no good writing a book for money. I'd sooner break in horses. When you break in horses you make something good out of something that could be bad. It's easy to turn out an outlaw but it's hard to give a horse—well, sort of . . . you know . . . character, say—make him work with you instead of against you.

"When I first met Peter Finlay he gave me a book called *My Brilliant Career*. He reckons a woman wrote it but she calls herself Miles Franklin. It's the best book I've ever read. She never baulks a fence. She's game, got heart. . . .

"I don't know . . . writing's funny . . . I don't think you see it right. You'd like to have a hell of a good time in a book you'd write. Now, that it . . . maybe, when you've been tossed a few times you'll see it my way."

We were sitting on the top rail of the horseyard looking at a colt he was mouthing. The horse champed at the heavy, mouthing bit. The corners of its mouth were red and raw.

"That colt's too long in the back," he said suddenly, then went on, "If a bloke gave you a hundred quid for a book you can bet your life it's his way, but if all the poor and suffering people raise their hats to you for writing it—that's different; it makes it worth while then. But you'll have to mix it with people first. You'll like them. We own this country and we'll make it a paradise. Men are equal here. Good luck to you, anyway," he added, "you write books. But take this job at Simmons's till you find your feet."

Mr. Simmons showed me an advertisement in the *Age* a few days later. A Business College in Melbourne was offering a scholarship for training in Accountancy to those who could pass an examination in History, Geography, Arithmetic and English, the papers for which would be sent to the local schoolmaster on application.

I wrote away for these papers and a week later Mr. Tucker told me they had arrived.

"You will notice, Marshall," he told me severely, as if I had made an accusation against him, "that the seal on these examination papers is intact. It is therefore impossible to tamper with the papers in any way. I have told William Foster about this examination and he will also be sitting for the scholarship. I'd like you to present yourself at the school at 10 a.m. sharp on Saturday morning. You may return to your seat."

William Foster was Tucker's pet and his star pupil. He could name all the Victorian rivers without drawing a breath and could do mental arithmetic with both hands on his head to show he didn't count with his fingers.

He curved a concealing arm round his exercise book when working and he was hard to copy from, but I had often managed it by jabbing him in the ribs when I wanted his arm removed.

His mother was very proud of him and told my mother that, only for him, I would never get a sum right.

When I met him outside the school on the Saturday morning I suggested we sit together for the examination, but he had his Sunday suit on and it infected his attitude towards me. He was stiff and unco-operative and told me his mother had said not to let me sit near him.

This was a blow but I followed him into school and sat beside him despite his efforts to shake me off.

Mr. Tucker observed my tactics and ordered me to the other end of the room where I sat looking through the window at Mt. Turalla, green and vivid in the sunshine. I was thinking of Joe and what a great day it was for rabbiting when Mr. Tucker rapped the desk and made an announcement.

"I am now about to break the seal securing the examination papers of Poulter's Business College," he said. "You will both note that the seal is intact."

He then snapped the string and withdrew the papers from the wrapping, keeping his cruel eyes on me as he did so.

For the next twenty minutes he sat reading the papers, sometimes frowning, sometimes raising his head and looking approvingly at William Foster who lowered his head in acknowledgment of this assurance.

I would like to have punched Tucker fair in the eye, then dashed away to Joe.

I was busy explaining to Joe exactly how I did it when Tucker handed us our papers. He glanced at the clock as he did so and said crisply, "It is now ten-thirty; you have till eleven-thirty to finish this paper."

I looked at the printed yellow sheet in front of me.

"Work out the compound interest on . . ."

Huh, this was easy . . .

"If ten men took . . ."

Cripes, proportion! This was a soda.

"A piece containing four acres three roods two perches . . ."
This was harder—hm!

I set to work while Tucker sat at his desk reading *The Field*, an English magazine with shiny pages.

I did not find the papers very hard, but when I compared my answers with William Foster after we left the schoolroom I concluded most of my answers were wrong, since they didn't agree with those given by William.

When I reached home I told father I had failed and he replied, "Never mind. You had a crack at it; that's the main thing."

A week before school broke up a long, brown envelope addressed to me came in the mail. It had been delivered to father and he was waiting in the kitchen with Mary and mother, for me to open it when I returned from school.

They gather round me as I broke the flap and pulled out the folded paper.

> Dear Sir,
>   We take pleasure in announcing that you have been awarded a full scholarship . . .

"I've got it!" I exclaimed unbelievingly, looking at them as if for an explanation.

"Show me," said father taking the letter from my hands.

"He's got it all right!" he exclaimed excitedly when he finished the letter. "Here, you read it." He handed the letter to mother. "Can you believe it! It says it all right. Fancy—a scholarship! Who would've thought as he'd've got a scholarship! I can't believe it." He turned and clapped my back. "Good on ya, son. You're a champion," then to mother, "What's the scholarship for, again? Let's look. What does it make him?"

"An accountant," said Mary, who was looking at the letter from above mother's shoulders. "An accountant has an office to himself and everything."

"Who's an accountant round here?" asked father, seeking enlightenment. "Would the bookkeeper in the big store at Balunga be an accountant, now?"

"No," said mother decidedly. "Of course not. He's a bookkeeper. Accountants have to be very clever."

"Mr. Bryan would be an accountant," said Mary. "He's the Secretary of the butter factory. Someone said he gets six pounds a week."

"If he gets that someone's a liar," said father decidedly. "I don't think the manager gets that. I'll go up and find out from him what this accountant really is. It sounds like our troubles are over, anyway. If Alan ever makes six quid a week he needn't call the king his uncle."

Father didn't waste any time. He saddled a horse and made for the factory. When he returned late in the afternoon he had further astounding news—William Foster had failed.

"It's right," father exclaimed, unable to hide his excitement. "I met Mrs. Foster and she told me—as if it were wonderful, mind you—that she had got a letter saying William could sit for the examination next year. You should've seen her when I told her about Alan—hell!

"And I saw Bryan, too," he went on. "You're right, Mary, he's an accountant all right. And he told me that top-ranking accountants can get over six quid a week though, you never know, he might be talking through his hat. Anyway, they look after the books of big companies—oil companies and places like that. When they become accountants they have letters after their name—wait till I see. I wrote them down on a piece of paper."

He fumbled in his pocket a moment then found the paper he was seeking. "Just a minute now. I wrote it down while Bryan was telling me. Here it is—L.I.C.A. and that means— I've got it here—Licentiate of the Institute of Commonwealth Accountants, whatever that is. There's not many blokes got it, so Bryan says. According to him it seems an important thing to get, those letters. . . ."

He looked at me approvingly. "I never thought I'd live to see the day that Alan has letters after his name."

On a sudden impulse he lifted me in his arms, big as I was, and gave me a hug.

He got drunk that night and came whooping home when we were all in bed, and I heard mother ask anxiously, "Any fights?"

"No," said father, "a couple of swings, that's all."

For the next week he and mother sat up late at night, talking and working out figures on paper, and I knew they were discussing my future.

"Mum and I have decided that we all shift to Melbourne, Alan," father told me one day. "It'll take us a while to fix things up, but when we do we'll pack up our swags and beat it. Your future is down there, not here. I'll get work; that'll be easy enough. And you can take a job in an office while you're learning how to be an accountant. Any office'd rush you when they knew you got a scholarship. Anyway, I'm not doing so well here now. And it'll get worse, what with the number of cars you see getting round. I must have seen eight or nine today." Then he added, "How do you feel about leaving here?"

"Good," I said. "I'll learn to be a writer the same time as I learn to be an accountant. It'll be great, I reckon."

"That's what I reckon," he said.

But when, alone, I thought it over, I suddenly felt that I could never leave the bush from which, in some strange way, I gained my strength. I had never seen a city. Now I saw it as some vast complex machine attended by hosts of L.I.C.A.'s with their ledgers and sunless faces. The thought depressed me and I sought out Joe who was setting traps in the bush behind his house.

When I told him we would soon be going away to live in Melbourne he looked thoughtfully at the trap in his hand and said, "You're a lucky cow; there's no doubt about it. But you always been lucky. Remember when you caught two rabbits in the one trap?"

"Yes," I answered, pleased with the memory.

We sat down together on the grass and talked about Melbourne and the trams that were there and the thousands of people and of how I would earn six pounds a week.

"The best thing about it," reflected Joe, "is that you'll be able to go to the museum any time you want to. They tell me there's everything there."

"I suppose so," I said. "I'll go there I suppose, but I want to write books. There's a big library in Melbourne. I'll go there, I reckon."

"You'll have to give up riding," said Joe. "A horse'll come down in Melbourne quicker than anywhere."

"Yes, that's the crook part about it," I said, feeling depressed again. "Anyway, trams take you where you want to go."

"I wonder how you'll get on with your crutches down there?" Joe mused. "The crowds an' that . . .?"

"Crutches!" I exclaimed, dismissing the inference contemptuously. "Crutches are nothing . . .!"